Passionate Action

Passionate Action

Yeats's Mastery of Drama

David Richman

Newark: University of Delaware Press
London: Associated University Presses

©2000 by Associated University Presses, Inc.

All rights reserved. Authorization to photocopy items for internal or personal use, or the internal or personal use of specific clients, is granted by the copyright owner, provided that a base fee of $10.00, plus eight cents per page, per copy is paid directly to the Copyright Clearance Center, 222 Rosewood Drive, Danvers, Massachusetts 01923.[0-87413–718–7/00 $10.00 + 8¢ pp, pc.] Other than as indicated in the foregoing, this book may not be reproduced, in whole or in part, in any form (except as permitted by Sections 107 and 108 of the U.S. Copyright Law, and except for brief quotes appearing in reviews in the public press).

Associated University Presses
440 Forsgate Drive
Cranbury, NJ 08512

Associated University Presses
16 Barter Street
London WC1A 2AH, England

Associated University Presses
P.O. Box 338, Port Credit
Mississauga, Ontario
Canada L5G 4L8

The paper used in this publication meets the requirements of the American National Standard for Permanence of Paper for Printed Library Materials Z39.48-1984.

Library of Congress Cataloging-in-Publication Data

Richman, David, 1951–
    Passionate action : Yeat's mastery of drama / David Richman.
       p. cm.
    Includes bibliographical references (p.) and index.
    ISBN 0–87413–718–7 (alk. paper)
    1. Yeats, W. B. (William Butler), 1865–1939—Dramatic works. 2. Verse drama, English—Irish authors—History and criticism. 3. Ireland—In literature. I. Title.

PR5909.D7 R53 2000
822'.8–dc21

00–023413

PRINTED IN THE UNITED STATES OF AMERICA

In Memory of My Parents
Sam Richman 1918–1964
Sylvia Richman Dickter 1916–1999

Contents

Acknowledgments	9
List of Abbreviations	11
Chronological List of Yeats's Plays	13
Introduction: Sightless Insights	17
1. The Problem of Personality	27
2. Writing for the Ear	59
3. Reshaping the Plot	86
4. Opinions and Ideas	121
5. The Playwright as Stage Machinist	152
A Note on Sources	185
Notes	187
Bibliography	193
Index	196

Acknowledgments

This book has been enriched by many collaborations, and in its making I have incurred numerous debts.

I wish to thank A. P. Watt Ltd. on behalf of Michael Yeats for permission to quote from the plays, poems and prose of W. B. Yeats, and I wish to thank Simon and Schuster for permission to quote from W. B. Yeats's *Collected Plays, Collected Poems, Autobiographies, Essays and Introductions, Explorations, Memoirs* and *Mythologies*.

A portion of chapter 1 originally appeared in *New England Theatre Journal,* and a portion of chapter 2 originally appeared in *Atenea*. I am grateful to Stuart Hecht of the *New England Theatre Journal* and to Nandita Batra of *Atenea* for permission to use this material. I also wish to thank Rick Friedman for permission to use the photograph on the cover. I am also indebted to a Summer Stipend from the National Endowment for the Humanities, as well as to an additional Summer Stipend from the College of Liberal Arts, University of New Hampshire.

The book began as a series of conversations about Yeats's plays with my friends and colleagues Jarold Ramsey, Jon Griffin, the late Jim Spenko and the late Jim Rieger. Their friendship illuminates these pages, and I hope that what I have to say about Yeats and the theatre does honor to the memory of Professor Rieger and Professor Spenko.

During recent years, the book and its author have been enriched by conversations about Yeats and other matters with John and Susan Edwards, David Andrew, Georgeann Murphy, Susan Goldin and Doug Tilton.

The community of Yeats scholars welcomed a novice attempting to make the leap from Shakespeare studies. I am especially grateful to the faculty and students of the 1997 Yeats International Summer School, Sligo, directed by Ron Schuchard. I owe thanks to the Yeats Society of Sligo for making my wife and me welcome to the school, and for graciously meeting the needs of a blind sojourner.

Warwick Gould, Sam and Joan McCready, Heinz Kosok, Janis Haswell, Jon Stalworthy and Ann Saddlemyer offered me advice and encouragement when these were most needed. I am especially grateful to Derek Chapman, in whose production of *The Countess Cathleen* I had the pleasure to participate, and from whom I learned a great deal about how Yeats really works in the theatre.

I could neither have prepared nor written this book without the assistance of many readers, all of them undergraduates at the University of New Hampshire. I take particular pleasure in thanking them: Jennifer Gilkie, Kim Bond, Allison Wiza, Dove Stuart, Shawna Forstrom, Marcus DelGreco, Christie Cloutier and Melany Kuchinski.

I am grateful to Donald Mell and the editors at the University of Delaware Press. Karen Druliner and Georgeann Murphy earn my profound gratitude for saving me from many errors, embarrassments and infelicities. All errors of fact, taste, judgment or style remaining in these pages are solely mine.

My children, Sam and Beatrice, gave skeptical interest to the project that absorbed so much of their father's attention. I would have lacked both the temerity to begin, and the strength to complete this book without the support and love of my wife, Susan. I hope that some of her informed passion for the theatre and for education has found its way into these pages.

List of Abbreviations

AU	W. B. Yeats, *Autobiographies* London: Macmillan, 1955.
CM	Augusta Gregory, *Cuchulain of Muirthemne* Coole Edition; New York: Oxford University Press, 1970; First published 1902.
CP	W. B. Yeats, *Collected Poems* London: Macmillan, 1961.
CPL	W. B. Yeats, *Collected Plays*, London: Macmillan, 1962.
E and I	W. B. Yeats, *Essays and Introductions*, London: Macmillan, 1961.
EXP	W. B. Yeats, *Explorations* London: Macmillan, 1962.
L	Allan Wade ed. *The Letters of W. B. Yeats* London: Hart-Davis, 1954.
M	W. B. Yeats, *Mythologies* London: Macmillan, 1959.
MEM	W. B. Yeats, *Memoirs* Ed. Denis Donoghue. New York: Macmillan, 1972.
VB	W. B. Yeats, *A Vision Reissue with the Author's Final Revisions* New York: Macmillan, 1965.
VPL	*The Variorum Edition of the Plays of W. B. Yeats* Ed. Russell K. Alspach, New York: Macmillan, 1966.

Chronological List of Yeats's Plays

Since Yeats was an inveterate reviser of his plays, preparing a chronological list is not a straightforward matter. On several plays, *The Countess Cathleen*, *The Shadowy Waters*, and *The Player Queen*, the playwright worked for many years, producing multiple drafts and variant versions. In the following list, I give dates of first performance, dates of completion or first publication if these differ significantly from dates of first performance, and dates of principal revisions. I do not include the plays completed prior to *The Countess Cathleen*, which Yeats chose not to include in his *Collected Plays*.

The Countess Cathleen first published 1892; first performed 1899; principal revisions 1911.

The Land of Heart's Desire first performed 1894.

1902 to 1910 were Yeats's most active years as a director of the Irish National Theatre which took up residence in 1904 in the newly opened Abbey Theatre. Many of the plays of these years were composed in collaboration with Augusta Gregory. Yeats noted in his *Collected Plays*, 1934, that Gregory had a hand wherever there is dialect, and often where there is not.

Cathleen ni Houlihan first performed 1902.

The Pot of Broth first performed 1902.

Where There is Nothing first performed 1902; (thoroughly rewritten and renamed *The Unicorn from the Stars* first performed 1907).

The Hourglass first performed 1903; principal revisions 1911–12, 1914.

The King's Threshold first performed 1903; principal revisions 1904–6, 1922.

The Shadowy Waters begun during the 1880's; first performed 1904; principal revisions 1905–6, 1911.

On Baile's Strand first performed 1904; principal revisions 1906.

Deirdre first performed 1906; principal revisions 1907–8.

The Green Helmet first performed 1910; (This superseded an earlier prose version, *The Golden Helmet*, first performed 1908).

The following four plays, intended for private performance, were published together as *Four Plays for Dancers* in 1921.

At the Hawk's Well first performed 1916.

The Dreaming of the Bones completed 1917; performed at the Abbey 1931.

The Only Jealousy of Emer completed 1919; performed at the Abbey 1926. (A prose adaptation of this play, *Fighting the Waves*, was performed at the Abbey in 1929 but was not included in the *Collected Plays*).

Calvary completed 1920; not performed during Yeats's lifetime.

Yeats's writing and production of plays continued steadily until his death in 1939.

The Player Queen begun 1907; first performed 1919; revised version published 1922.

The Cat and the Moon completed 1917; performed at the Abbey 1926.

Sophocles' *King Oedipus* first performed 1927.

Sophocles' *Oedipus at Colonus* first performed 1928.

The Resurrection first published 1927; revised version published 1932; first performed 1934.

The Words Upon the Window Pane first performed 1930.

The King of the Great Clock Tower first performed 1934.

A Full Moon in March completed 1935; not performed during Yeats's lifetime.

The Herne's Egg completed 1937; not performed during Yeats's lifetime.

Purgatory first performed 1938.

The Death of Cuchulain completed 1939; not performed during Yeats's lifetime.

Introduction: Sightless Insights

> *A living man is blind and drinks his drop;*
> . . . .
> *I am content to live it all again*
> *And yet again, if it be life to pitch*
> *Into the frog-spawn of a blind man's ditch;*
> *A blind man battering blind men.*
> —*"A Dialogue of Self and Soul"*

In Yeats's last play *The Death of Cuchulain,* the eponymous legendary Irish hero receives six mortal wounds and has himself bound to a standing stone so that he may die upon his feet. An acquisitive blind man enters, the same blind chicken- and bread-stealer who had appeared in another Cuchulain play, *On Baile's Strand*. The blind man has been told that he will be given twelve pennies if he fetches the great Cuchulain's head. Kneeling before the wounded man, he gropes up the body, past the knees, thighs, and waist, feeling for the neck. As he does this, Cuchulain speaks: "I think that you know everything, blind man; / My mother or my nurse said that the blind / Know everything." The blind man, his inner eye on the main chance, replies: "No, but they have good sense. / How could I have got twelve pennies for your head / If I had not good sense?" (CPL 444).

Being both blind and skeptical of the idea of the blind seer-saint, I find this character a useful corrective. Yeats's bracing, unsentimental depictions of the blind range from the prophet Tiresias to Cuchulain's nameless killer, and they demonstrate, among other things, that the life of the blind is a continuous collaboration. The Fool in *On Baile's Strand* remarks to his blind companion: "I would never be able to steal anything if you didn't tell me where to look for it" (CPL 161). The Blind Man, unable himself to look, must trade his special knowledge for the loan of the Fool's eyes. Since I am always borrowing other people's eyes in my difficult, daily negotiations with my blindness, I am drawn to Yeats's acerbic dramatizations of the collaborative relationship.

Yeats likely endorsed Synge's famous proposition that all art is a collaboration, but he also wrote that

> All creation requires one mind to make and one mind for enjoyment. The theater can at rare moments create this one mind for an hour or so, but this grows always more difficult. (MEM 215)

Inside and outside the theater, Yeats spent his creative life striving to bring his mind into unity with those of his many collaborators—with actors, dancers, designers—supremely with Augusta Gregory on folklore and plays and with George Yeats on *A Vision*.

My blindness requires me to engage continuously in difficult collaboration. I rage against my body's limits that make collaboration necessary, and I concomitantly value my fellow theater artists with whom I collaborate. This personal history gives me special insight into Yeats's many collaborations—both into the value he placed upon them and into his rage at their necessity. Coping with poor eyesight, he often dictated letters, and he occasionally asked others—Gregory, Pound, George Yeats—to read to him. One can imagine his gratitude for their help in conflict with his chafing because he needed it.

Yeats's life in the theater was a protracted struggle, and he famously lashed out at "The day's war with every knave and dolt / Theatre business, management of men" (CP 104). James Flannery observes that Yeats's "difficulties with actors were notorious."[1] But toward the end of his life, Yeats wrote that, though he wore out his youth in pursuit of his theatrical dream, his best friends were made for him by his plays. He memorialized

> William Fay at the end of *On Baile's Strand*, Mrs. Patrick Campbell in my *Deirdre*, passionate and solitary, and in later years that great artist Ninette de Valois in *Fighting the Waves*. These things will, it may be, haunt me on my deathbed. (EXP 416)

J. M. Synge and Augusta Gregory, his fellow directors of the Abbey Theatre, were always present in his thought and art. When he accepted the Nobel Prize he remarked that "two forms should have stood one at either side of me—an old woman sinking into the infirmity of age and a young man's ghost" (AU 374). Gregory did not react to her tribute in Yeats's Nobel speech with unmixed pleasure, wishing he had said "fighting the infirmity of age."[2]

This fit of pique may point to a deeper fissure in Yeats's relation with his closest theatrical collaborator and dearest friend. Generous as he was in his many tributes to Gregory, he was strangely reluctant to acknowledge her as coauthor of plays, chief among them *Cathleen ni Houlihan*, that bore his name alone. Gregory's claim on the play Yeats had come to believe was his most popular theatrical success may have surfaced when, to her coauthor's icy dissatisfaction, she performed the title role in a 1919 Abbey revival.[3] Thus conflict proved an element even in Yeats's closest theatrical friendship.

Yeats's career as theater manager, theater theorist, and playwright was full of battle. He took unexampled pleasure in the fusion of words, music, rhythm, dance, mask. At the same time, he often railed against the visual dimension of the theater. Thrusting against every theatrical current of his time, he fiercely advocated the word as the theater's most important element. Early in his career, when the Abbey Theatre was a far-off dream, he wrote that "The theater began in ritual, and it cannot come to its greatness again without recalling words to their ancient sovereignty" (E and I 170). His theatrical career can be described as a prolonged struggle to create a countertruth to the technically elaborate, ever more spectacular theater that he perceived to be dominant in Europe and America.

Amid the voluminous theoretical and critical writings on the modern and contemporary theater—with their unremitting praise for movement, gesture, dance, backdrop, inarticulate sound—above all with their frightening distrust of the word—I find continued support and nourishment in Yeats's vision of a theater in which the playwright's words, passionately and clearly spoken, are indeed sovereign. I find an ally in this theater director who insists on stilling the stage's restlessness and on commanding his audience to give ear. Yet always in conflict even over his most firmly held theatrical principles, he did not achieve full dramatic maturity until he halfdiscovered, half-invented a kind of theater at whose center moved a wordless dancer. Yeats's embattled relation with the theater is illustrated by the fact that this most insistent advocate of the word formed two of his most successful collaborative partnerships with dancers who did not utter a syllable as they performed in his plays. Michio Itow danced the well's silent guardian in *At the Hawk's Well*, 1916, and Ninette de Valois danced both the silent Fand in *Fighting the Waves*, 1929, and the silent queen in *The King of the Great Clock Tower*, 1934.

Through years of toil, Yeats perfected a form of theater in which the verse speaker and the dancer are partners. In the plays he composed and produced between 1916 and his death in 1939, this playwright for dancers established himself as the most significant verse dramatist writing in English since Shakespeare's time. T. S. Eliot famously acknowledged the debt that all subsequent verse dramatists owe to Yeats: "Yeats had nothing, and we have had Yeats. . . . I do not know where our debt to him as a dramatist ends, and in time it will not end until that drama itself ends."[4] Does the fact of my blindness constrain me to join Yeats in asserting the power and primacy of the word in an art many of whose theorists from Craig through Artaud to Grotowski assert that the word is growing ever less important? I hold with Yeats the minority position that the power and pleasure afforded by the dance of strong syllables, by the words in their intricate rhythmic patterns spoken from a stage and listened to by an audience is unlike, and cannot be replaced by, other theatrical pleasures or sources of theatrical power.

I also know as did Yeats that in the theater, as in the life some argue theater imitates, listening is not enough. In the best of all possible worlds, the eye and the ear collaborate—in the audience as well as in collaborating theater artists. Both senses must be appealed to, and the pleasure taken by each sense enriches the pleasure taken by the other. But however keen to the beauty and power of the dance and the mask, Yeats never lost sight of the fact that the eye and the ear are often at war with each other in the theater. The modern theater, as he diagnosed it, was restless, nervous, full of extraneous movement and spectacle, never allowing for that slowing and stilling that permit tragic reverie. "I wanted to get rid of irrelevant movement; the stage must become still that words might keep all their vividness, and I wanted vivid words" (E and I 527). He took pleasure in Sarah Bernhardt, whose pristine economy of gesture and movement he memorably described (EXP 87). Yeats's visual effects were always the servants of the spoken play, never its masters. He always advocated the poet over the performer, and he always advocated the performer over the designer. He argued that too close an attention to what the eye sees daily can be a distraction from the inner vision at which the theater aims.

"A Funeral Elegy," possibly composed by Shakespeare in 1612, develops this idea in somber stanzas. (Although the authorship of this poem is a matter of continuing controversy, I am convinced the lines are Shakespeare's, and I am heartened by the thought that these two verse dramatists would have found themselves in agreement on this point.) Yeats did not know this poem, but he would have agreed with lines that give precise expression to a principle he would apply all his life to the composition and production of plays.

> The willful blindness that hoodwinks the eyes
> Of men enwrapped in an earthy veil
> Makes them most ignorantly exercise
> And yield to humor when it doth assail,
> Whereby the candle and the body's light
> Darkens the inward eyesight of the mind,
> Presuming still it sees, even in the night
> Of that same ignorance which makes them blind.[5]

Yeats became what Katharine Worth describes as a dramatist of the interior.[6] The imagination to which his plays appeal is nourished by that which the outward eye does not see. Every traveller in this inward world is uncertain, so it is a world in which I need be no more uncertain than any other traveller. Since my travels in the outward world are full of uncertainty, I am naturally drawn by Yeats's inward world and by his strong championing of inward vision. For Yeats, the primary sense through which this inward vision is achieved is the ear, and the mind behind it. In "The Mother of God," a late lyric poem, Yeats conjures "a fallen flare / Through the hollow of an ear." In his note to these lines, he describes "Byzantine mosaic pictures of the Annunciation, which show a line drawn from a star to the ear of the virgin. She received the word through the ear, a star fell, and a star was born" (CP 536). This description, to apply the sacred to the profane, is apposite to the effect of a verse play upon its hearers.

Yeats's insistence on the ear as the primary sense to which plays appeal renders him out of fashion and out of date in the world of twentieth-century theater. One has to go back to Ben Jonson for similar admonitions that the audience must "hear, not see a play."[7] Yeats's imperative to write for the ear set him at odds with theatrical modernists like his sometime collaborator Gordon Craig, who insisted that plays must appeal primarily to the spectators' keen and questioning eyes.[8] This theatrical verse modernist paradoxically harked back to the plays of Sophocles and Racine, even as he strove to create a theater that, sixty years after his death, still seems ahead of its time. Sylvia Ellis, responding to James Flannery's 1991 Abbey production of *A Full Moon in March* (first published in 1935) notes that

> it is quite understandable that even those who were familiar with Yeats's plays and knew what to expect should still today risk being shocked. Students of Yeats may tend to forget that his dramatic works, particularly his dance plays such as *A Full Moon in March*, have not lost their power as avant-garde innovation and the relentless demands that they make on their audiences have not weakened through time.[9]

Students of Yeats have long been familiar with the battles that plagued him and with which he plagued others during his years with the Abbey. Roy Foster aptly titles a chapter in his 1997 biography of Yeats "Delighting in Enemies," and he quotes George Russell, one of the playwright's oldest and most sorely tried friends: "It is very unfortunate that Yeats should arouse such savage enmities among people who long ago had every inclination to serve him."[10]

Yeats battled with a like ferocity against the drama itself. The central paradoxes in his theatrical career point to the chief sources of conflict. This most passionate advocate of the word's primacy composed plays for wordless dancers. The poet who raged against anything that broke upon his artist's solitude needed and valued many collaborators, while holding even the dearest of them at a wary distance. The shocking modernist adhered to the most ancient theatrical forms—was more an Aristotelian than an Artaudian.

The playwright's forty years in the theater can best be described as an agon: a struggle for mastery against a form and a set of conventions that he both adored and loathed. Yeats battled to make himself into a playwright. He was not a natural dramatist. He slowly and painfully taught himself the arts of the theater—shaping them the while to his own purposes. As with words, he was a fierce traditionalist in many of the theater's arts. This translator of Sophocles thought of drama in terms of its Aristotelian elements: plot, character, dialogue, thought—in an age when other modernists were calling these into question. Yeats's adherence to traditional dramatic forms imposed upon his dramaturgy a necessary discipline—a word he valued—as dependable and certain as the discipline imposed by the contrapuntal relations between meter and rhythm. As he never abandoned meter in verse, he never abandoned the Aristotelian elements in drama.

Yet he waged epic battle with each of those elements. He hated the long labor of shaping and reshaping the plot. The business of putting plays on the stage wearied him. He deplored the expression of opinion in drama, knowing at the same time that thought, as well as action, is necessary to tragedy. Most of all, he hated "character" as that term was understood by most of his theatrical contemporaries and immediate predecessors. The following chapters attempt to trace the conflicts through which he transmuted the traditional elements of drama and fused them to create a wholly modern theater that still exerts its influence upon contemporary playwrights. Like most of the beginners Aristotle mentions, Yeats the apprentice playwright mastered character and diction before making gains in his protracted struggles with plot and thought. Following the road the evolving dramatist took, I will discuss the dramatic elements, not in their order of Aristotelian importance, but in the order that mirrors Yeats's development.

From his father, he had absorbed a principle that was to actuate his dramatic writing. "All must be an idealization of speech, and at some moment of passionate action or somnambulistic reverie" (AU 42). So great was his need to create passionate action and to communicate it to an audience that he undertook the immense and often thankless labor of making himself into a dramatist. Through myriad setbacks and failures, he attained sufficient mastery over the ancient elements of drama to enable him to fashion a new and difficult form of theater.

He expected most audiences and critics to chafe at his plays' difficulties. "In writing these little plays, I knew that I was creating something which could only fully succeed in a civilisation very unlike ours" (VPL 566). But he also knew that, under the right circumstances, his plays could give those "moments of excitement that are the dramatist's reward" (CP 536). Such excitement rises when a theater full of people hear or see a passionate personality: Emer renouncing Cuchulain's love forever, or the silent queen dancing in erotic frenzy with a severed head. Though Aristotle called plot the soul of tragedy, Yeats departed from Aristotle in considering plot a most necessary means to an end. The end of drama, the reason for Yeats's long struggle to master it, was the creation of personality caught in its moment of passionate action.

Passionate Action

1
The Problem of Personality

> *But actors lacking music*
> *Do most excite my spleen,*
> *They say it is more human*
> *To shuffle, grunt and groan,*
> *Not knowing what unearthly stuff*
> *Rounds a mighty scene.*
> —*"The Old Stone Cross"*

In one of his numerous attempts to define personality and distinguish it from character, Yeats wrote his father that,

> Juliet has personality; her nurse has character. I look upon personality as the individual form of our passion.... I probably get the distinction from the stage, where we say a man is a "character actor" meaning that he builds up a part out of observation, or we say that he is "an emotional actor" meaning that he builds it up out of himself. And in this last case we always add, if he is not commonplace, that he has personality. (L 549)

Yeats's career as a playwright can be described as a series of attempts to keep the pushing world at a distance so that his figures, untrammeled by external circumstance, can give individual form to their passion. He was annoyed by conventional character acting, believing it to vitiate the tragic ecstasy at which he aimed: "I found that when English actors play my work, they have a habit of comedy. Always at the noble moment, the great moment, when the actor must speak thinking lyrically and musically, these were the very moments when he desired to characterize. And out of this there has arisen on the English stage a perpetual over-emphasis.... It is pseudo-comedy instead of tragedy."[1]

Cathleen ni Houlihan first performed 1902

The chief figure in *Cathleen ni Houlihan* provides a nearly perfect example of what the playwright meant by personality, in that she gives an individual form to passion. Her language, her expression, her mode of being, are unique to herself. In this brief, disturbing play, whose action is set in 1798 on the eve of a failed Irish rebellion against the occupying British, a mysterious old woman wanders into a cottage where a wedding is being planned. The old woman's passion is defined by the motive of freeing Ireland from foreign tyranny or, as she herself expresses it, the "hope of getting my beautiful fields back again; the hope of putting the strangers out of my house" (VPL 226). As Yeats made clear in his prefatory note to the play (VPL 232), Cathleen was not built up out of observation. Like the actor of personality whom he was to describe in his letter to his father, the poet built this figure up out of himself.

As she rehearsed the role, Maud Gonne discovered as well that she could not build up the part out of observation, nor could she rely on conventional modes of theatrical expression like those urged on her by George Moore. Her letter to Yeats written in March, 1902, makes clear her reaction to Moore's suggestions

> which would have entirely changed the character of the play and which I think would have spoiled it. For instance, he wanted Cathleen to get up when she talked about her beautiful green fields and to walk to the door and come back again. In fact, he wanted her to be wandering round the cottage all the time and make most of her remarks from the front of the stage instead of from the corner of the fire. I don't agree with Moore at all about this, for I think one must keep up the idea of the poor old weary woman who would certainly sit down and rock herself over the fire, and not get up and walk about until the idea of meeting her friends comes to her.[2]

In bringing Cathleen to life on the stage, both Yeats and Gonne understood that she must appear more than the ordinary old woman, marshalling Ireland's young men to battle. Rocking by the fire, crooning her cryptic and disturbing songs of sacrifice and memory, she exemplified what Yeats was to call "personality," while what he was to call "character" was exemplified by the members of the Gillane family.

1 / THE PROBLEM OF PERSONALITY

During his most active years with the Irish National Theatre (1902–10), Yeats often attempted in essays, letters, journal entries, and lectures to distinguish personality from character, and to account for the difficulties of presenting personality on the modern stage. During those same years, the Hungarian critic Georg Lukacs, whom Thomas Mann was to describe as the finest critic of modern times, was reaching similar conclusions in "The Sociology of Modern Drama," first published in 1909. Lukacs is the only other major writer during the first half of the twentieth century to deal at length with the modern theater's inability to express unique personality. Employing a different vocabulary and different tools of analysis, he reached strikingly similar conclusions to Yeats's. The one important difference was that Lukacs, a theorist, simply declared the theater to be moribund, and prophesied that the century's most important writing would be done in other forms. Yeats, the practitioner, set about to reshape the theater. Although Yeats and Lukacs were not aware of each other's work, the Hungarian provides a useful yardstick against which to measure the Irishman's theory and practice. *Cathleen ni Houlihan*, a play unknown to Lukacs, eerily illustrates one of his important conclusions: "For the stage is turned into the point of intersection for pairs of worlds distinct in time—the realm of drama is one where past and future, 'no longer' and 'not yet,' come together in a single moment."[3]

The old woman's tragic power derives in large part from her embodiment of Ireland's heroic past and from her concomitant ability to perceive a future free of tyrannizing strangers. Like Gonne, Yeats rejected Moore's suggestion that Cathleen walk up and down in front of the footlights so as to dominate the stage. His description of the sort of impression he wanted her to make anticipates Lukacs's formulation. "She looks far ahead and far backward, and cannot be excited in that sense—or rather she will be a less poetical personage if she is" (L 367).

Maud Gonne's performance as Cathleen ni Houlihan had a profound and lasting effect on the play's initial audiences. For Yeats, Gonne remained the ideal against whom all other actresses assaying the role could never measure up. Her "great height made Cathleen seem a divine being fallen into our mortal infirmity. Since then, the part has been twice played in America by women who insisted on keeping their young faces; and one of these, as she came to the door, dropped her cloak, as I have been told, and showed a white satin dress embroidered with shamrocks." (VPL 233) The tendency of conventional performers to characterize just at those moments when passionate lyricism is most needed, which Yeats would decry throughout his career, is grotesquely exemplified by that shamrock-covered dress. Gonne's costume, by contrast, had consisted of "a beautiful untidy grey wig, a torn grey flannel dress exactly like the old women wear in the west, bare feet, and a big blue hooded cloak. You would give me a penny in the street if you saw me, and I look sixty at least."[4]

The play's action is simple. The poor old woman who gives individual form to Ireland's passion for independence from England persuades young Michael Gillane to abandon his bride-to-be for an almost certain death in what the audience knows will be a losing battle. She does not exhort the young man to follow her, employing what Yeats was to describe as the "commonplace will," the "business will" (L 441). Instead, she virtually hypnotizes him with the intensity of her passion and the inexorability of its expression.

> **OLD WOMAN** (who is standing in the doorway.) They are wondering that there were songs made for me; there have been many songs made for me. I heard one on the wind this morning. (sings)
>
>> Do not make a great keening
>> When the graves have been dug to-morrow.
>> Do not call the white-scarfed riders
>> To the burying that shall be to-morrow.
>> Do not spread food to call strangers
>> To the wakes that shall be to-morrow.
>> Do not give money for prayers
>> For the dead that shall die to-morrow. . . .
>
> They will have no need of prayers, they will have no need of prayers.
> **MICHAEL** I do not know what that song means, but tell me something I can do for you.
>
> (VPL 228)

She penetrates the young man's consciousness chiefly by means of her songs, and these songs provide early examples of the lyric expression of passionate personality in the theater for which Yeats strove throughout his dramatic career. Compelled by the power of the old woman's tragic lyricism, Michael rushes from his house and his bride. Young Patrick, gazing at Cathleen, sees not an old woman but a young girl with the "walk of a queen" (VPL 230). At its close, the play adumbrates a future of tragic exaltation.

1 / THE PROBLEM OF PERSONALITY

Cathleen ni Houlihan's power over its original audiences was due in large measure to factors extrinsic to the play: Ireland's political and cultural aspirations, and the presence of Maud Gonne, the very personification of the figure she portrayed, in the cast. Shaw's remark, "*A Doll's House* will be as flat as ditchwater when *A Midsummer Night's Dream* will still be as fresh as paint; but it will have done more work in the world,"⁵ can be applied as well to the play first performed in Dublin under British rule in 1902. Yet it remains a mark of the play's authentic power that it was able to focus upon itself so many disparate political and cultural elements. Whatever its other virtues and shortcomings, it indicated Yeats's way of giving lyric expression to the passion of personality in the theater.

At the play's conception, Cathleen ni Houlihan, who personified Ireland, was linked with Maud Gonne, who came to personify Cathleen. Thus Gonne, who inspired so much in Yeats's work, demonstrated the manner of expressing personality on the stage that he was to follow through all his plays. Indeed, it is instructive to read one of Yeats's later descriptions of her ability, by sheer force of personality, to sway a crowd. In *The Trembling of the Veil* (1922), Yeats described Gonne in 1897, the year of the Jubilee riots. The figure he there limned stands as a prototype for all of the figures—Seanchan, Cuchulain, Deirdre, Emer, Dervorgilla, Swift, and of course Cathleen ni Houlihan—to whose passion Yeats sought to give individual form in his plays.

> Her beauty, backed by her great stature, could instantly affect an assembly, and not, as often with our stage beauties, because obvious and florid, for it was incredibly distinguished. And if, as must be that it might seem that assembly's very self, fused unified and solitary, her face, like the face of some Greek statue, showed little thought, her whole body seemed a masterwork of long labouring thought. (AU 242–43)

Yeats conjures—as he does with increasing force throughout his theoretical, critical, and autobiographical writings—an ideal for the expression of passion on the stage. That ideal emerges as a noble, unified being, communicating in all its lineaments the individual form of its passion. Yeats adhered to this ideal, perhaps first suggested by the spectacle of Maud Gonne in the 1890s, throughout his long career.

Gonne's acting in the role of Cathleen ni Houlihan, Yeats's first fully successful assay in the lyric expression of personality on the stage, serves as an emblem whose appropriateness and power the dramatist would have been the first to recognize. Yet, even though Gonne was necessary to the creation of this play, she was not necessary to its continued success. Una Ellis-Fermor, who has written as well about drama and theater as anyone in our century, recalled in 1939, shortly after Yeats's death, the impression made on her by a London performance of the play. Her description is worth quoting at length, because it provides strong evidence of the play's tragic power, even when an actress other than Maud Gonne took the title role.

> It must have been in part, at least, an audience of Englishmen or Anglo-Irishmen that saw *Cathleen ni Houlihan* that day with Miss Sarah Allgood in the part of Cathleen. A play was a real thing to me in those days, as no play alas can ever be again, and I remember now recoiling from the wildness and the violence, the old woman with her boding, bringing her talk of war and death into the midst of ordinary things. . . . There was something as yet terrifying and savage about people who talked familiarly about it in the everyday setting of a homely cottage. The average Anglo-Irishman in the audience, meeting the play as most did for the first time, recoiled vigourously upon his English blood. Then came the quickening all over the stage, the exaltation that was the secret of a people. . . .
> "They that have red cheeks will have pale cheeks for my sake, and for all that, they will think they are well paid.
> They shall be remembered forever;
> They shall be alive forever;
> They shall be speaking forever;
> The people shall hear them forever."
> I think that then the Anglo-Irish part of the audience suffered that strange experience, the penetration and irradiation of the mind by something that appears to alter its constitution or its orientation and is called conversion. I can remember as if it were yesterday the swing over of sympathy, more sudden and complete than in any other play I have seen, the releasing of exaltation and vision as the world of Edwardian London, in which we had till then been reared was, suddenly, no longer "solid under the footsole."[6]

Even outside Ireland and even without Gonne, the play held its audience in tragic ecstasy. Yeats's ability to give lyric expression on the stage to a unique personality was and remains a chief source of the play's power.

But, of course, it was not Yeats's play. Tragic terror arises because Cathleen's passionate reverie is set against a precise, circumstantial depiction of ordinary country life. In Yeats's prefatory letter to Lady Gregory published with the play, he acknowledged his inability to show such ordinary life on the stage, and he gave a partial account of the collaboration out of which the play had grown (VPL 232).

This life is depicted by means of precise, circumstantial prose dialogue and by the comedy that arises from details of ordinary characterization. Peter Gillane's reaction to the sudden infusion of money that the marriage will bring about, young Patrick's desire for a greyhound, and Bridget's hope that her younger son will become a priest. As James Pethica demonstrates, Augusta Gregory is entirely responsible for the way the Gillanes are depicted. She, not Yeats, brings their life to the stage. Her dramatic skill causes Cathleen's passionate reverie to mix so disturbingly and with such unforgettable effect into the Gillanes' hopes. The depiction of the family is her unaided work. Without Gregory's dramatization of the family's attempts to question and understand their strange guest, the unforgettable "swing over of sympathy" would not have been possible. Gregory's relation to Yeats in the writing of this play is most comparable to Beaumont's relation to Fletcher.[7]

Once again this play, produced seven years before Lukacs published his work on drama and which the Hungarian almost certainly did not know, illustrates one of his conclusions about the modern drama: "In the new drama, not merely passions are in conflict, but ideologies—*Weltanschauungen* as well. Because men collide who come from differing situations, value judgments must necessarily function as importantly at least as purely individual characteristics."[8] In creating the Gillanes, Augusta Gregory demonstrated her understanding, probably surpassing Yeats's, that Cathleen's tragic power would spring from her fundamental difference in ideology from the aspiring family whose small world the old woman was disturbing. The dramatic representation of this ideological conflict depended on Gregory's detailed portrayal of the Gillanes' economic and social circumstances.

Yet Yeats repeatedly and strenuously argued in essays and lectures that such depiction of the detail of ordinary life could hamper or limit the expression of tragic passion on the stage. Pronouncements against playwrights' realistic portrayals of character, and against the most common modes of character acting, are found throughout his writing. In an open letter to Augusta Gregory written in 1919, he defined passion as the straining of one's being against some obstacle that obstructs its unity (EXP 252). Obstructing that unity of being for which Yeats strove in the creation of his chief stage figures, as in all his work, were the habits and gestures of a conventional theatricality that had replaced ancient form. A break with form, a too close concern with intricacy and detail, a reliance on habit, characteristic, tendency—terms Yeats used pejoratively in his writings on the theater—all of these were antithetical to the expression in tragedy of passionate personality, fused and unified.

While Yeats was struggling to maintain ancient tragic form, often to the annoyance or anger of his Abbey audiences, Lukacs was reaching similar conclusions about the problem of portraying personality on the modern stage:

> An objective abstraction, capital, becomes the true productive agent in capitalist economy, and it scarcely has an organic relation with the personality of its accidental owner. Indeed, personality may often become superfluous, as in corporations. . . . The drama comes to be built upon mathematics—a complicated web of abstractions—and in this perspective character achieves significance merely as an intersection.[9]

What was for Lukacs a matter of historical necessity remained for Yeats an urgent cause to rage and lament. He singled out John Galsworthy's urban tragedy *Justice*, playing in London in 1910, as an illustration of everything that was wrong with the new drama of external circumstance. Had Lukacs known *Justice* he might have used it as the perfect illustration of the new drama of milieu.

> When you get to *Justice* you get to a play in which human life is simplified away to almost nothing. . . . The characterization is of the most external kind. But you have marvelous pictures of the prison cell, of *things*. . . . Human life is fading and dwindling away in a vast play of circumstance.[10]

Typical of this circumstantial, external expression of character was a wildly applauded scene in which an actor had to beat on a prison door. "One wondered that the actor was called for. Anybody could beat on a door in the dark. . . . If the actors had all died, we could have found other actors to do it just as well."[11]

Augusta Gregory recognized, as Yeats did not, that passionate personality would succeed on the modern stage only if it was grounded in credible external circumstance. A play of lyric passion divorced from circumstance, such as *The Shadowy Waters*, would fail as drama; a play of circumstance lacking in personality, such as *Justice*, would succeed. In the play on which Yeats and Gregory collaborated, tragic irony results from the terribly widening gap between the family's understanding of the poor old woman beside their fire and the audience's growing apprehension of her power. The lyric expression of that power and the manner of its presentation on stage were largely Yeats's contributions to the play, but Cathleen's dream of passion earns much of its theatrical effectiveness through contrast with the Gillanes to whom Augusta Gregory gave life and form. That Gregory is the coauthor of this play provides the best evidence for the critical commonplace that, whatever the merit in individual scenes and speeches, Yeats's shunning of the details of ordinary life, his failure to provide a ground of human circumstance, a credible milieu, from which his chief figures could mount in passionate reverie diminished the dramatic effectiveness of his early Abbey plays. Working together, he and Gregory had solved what Lukacs believed to be the central problem of modern drama. They had fused the expression of personality with the modes of ordinary character and circumstance, and they had made a lyric tragedy that was also a popular dramatic success. Yeats would not again achieve unmixed success as a poetic tragedian until he at last mastered the difficult art of fusing character, entangled in its web of circumstance, with personality.

The case for the shortcomings in Yeats's Abbey plays is put most compellingly by one of his earliest critics. L. A. G. Strong, in an essay published the year after Yeats's death, wrote as follows about the persons in the plays:

> The man to whom symbol and what it represents are almost in the nature of cause and effect, the man, that is to say, for whom the symbol is constant and will always call up its appropriate picture and emotion, will not always be at sufficient pains to embody his characters before an audience. The character will already be what he is to represent before he steps upon the stage. He will be a mask, his face already fixed in the appropriate grimace of mirth or grief. Shakespeare's characters are revealed, not presented. The very quality which is a strength to Yeats's poetry weakened his drama.[12]

Strong's assessment was echoed by Richard Ellmann in remarks about the pre-Noh Abbey plays.

> His dramas show the effect of much theorizing. The author's ideas about his characters dominate them, and the subject matter of *On Baile's Strand, The King's Threshold,* and *Deirdre* is all too human to allow for this kind of treatment. In spite of his principle of common language and common passion, his personages are close to arrangements and abstractions, and even in tragic circumstances, do not assume altogether human life. Something seems to be wrong with their breathing. They suffer, especially in *Deirdre,* from an overdose of royal blood, and in the other plays also, they are too often lopsided. Yeats has come close to a tragedy of humors. . . . He was soon to use masks to achieve enough distance from life so that his characters would not demand so pressingly as in the Irish legends to be entirely human. In his earlier treatment however, we feel an equivocation between formalized and realistic drama.[13]

As early as 1906, Yeats had become convinced that too much attention to the intricacy and detail of ordinary life could drain the humanity out of his dramatis personae. He writes, "When one constructs, bringing one's characters into complicated relationships with one another, something impersonal comes into the story" (E and I 273). Yeats was dangerously disagreeing with Aristotle, who urged dramatists to bring their characters into just the sort of relations that the apprentice Irish playwright was trying to avoid:

> If you string together a set of speeches expressive of character, and well finished in point of diction and thought, you will not produce the essential tragic effect nearly so well as with a play which, however deficient in these respects, yet has a plot and artistically constructed incidents.[14]

Paradoxically, Yeats in most of his early Abbey plays created an abstract, inhuman drama precisely because he sought to shun those elements that he judged would lead to its creation.

One of Yeats's core beliefs was that great drama required the expression of the whole personality, an expression distorted and muted by too much attention to intricate external circumstance. He held up as an ideal a performance of Sicilian *comedia* players, contrasting them with the performers of Galsworthy's *Justice,* a play he continued to disparage. The Sicilians did the right thing because their instincts are right. The other is an art of a complex period, where people do nothing right unless they are taught to do it, intonation by intonation, movement by movement. You felt also as you looked at the Sicilians that these players were showing their whole natures. They had confidence in themselves—they poured themselves out. You felt they went home exhausted because they had expressed themselves so completely. In the other, you felt the player was using only a little of himself; he was depressed. You watched him with a feeling of depression.[15]

Yeats sought an art which, like *comedia*, would bring about the joyous and complete expression of personality. He wanted his figures, like the Sicilian performers, to reveal their natures in their every passionate word, gesture, and expression.

He did come slowly to realize, in spite of his principles, that the depiction on the stage of ordinary character enmeshed in its web of circumstance provided necessary ground for his lyric expressions of mounting passion. In a note published with *Cathleen ni Houlihan* he acknowledged that accurate observation and imitation were important tools for any performer. "I cannot imagine this play or any folk play of our school acted by players with no knowledge of the peasant, and of the awkwardness and stillness of bodies that have followed the plough" (VPL 233). But as his theory of the expression of personality took shape, he insisted not on synthesizing, but on separating observation from vision. In his 1919 open letter to Augusta Gregory, he distinguished between two essentially different sorts of artists: "We stand on the margin between wilderness and wilderness, that which we observe through our senses and that which we can experience only, and our art is always the description of one or the other" (EXP 250–51). In this manifesto, Yeats perceived that the writers for the Abbey were at their most successful and truly useful when their minds, like clear mirrors, reflected the life that they could understand and see. He argued that those writers, their minds like smoking lamps, who could only feel and imagine should leave the theater before they turned it from its honesty. By this time in his career, he had temporarily left the Abbey as playwright, and his plays for dancers were intended for private performance.

But there is a widening fissure in Yeats's theory of personality on the stage—an internal conflict in his evolving approach to the composition of plays. Set against the strong bias in favor of inner experience to be found throughout Yeats's writings, one can detect an equally strong adherence to outward observation. Most memorably in such poems as "Byzantium," "A Dialogue of Self and Soul," and supremely in the final stanza of "The Circus Animals' Desertion," the champion of inner vision proclaims that the disordered and often vulgar welter of mundane detail is a necessary element in the lyric expression of tragic passion. Yeats was never more firmly on the side of inner experience, as opposed to the observation of ordinary life, than when he was inventing his new form of drama inspired by his readings with Pound of the Noh plays in Fenollosa's papers. In "Certain Noble Plays of Japan," the essay that most fully described this new sort of drama, he advocated the smoking lamp of inner experience, as opposed to the clear mirror of observation. Yet there is nothing more emblematic of Yeats's two minds about the efficacy of observation, even in drama based on visionary experience, than the fact that he accompanied Michio Itow, the dancer who played the Guardian of the Well in the first production in 1916 of *At the Hawk's Well*, and Edmund Dulac, who designed the costumes and masks for that production, on visits to the London Zoo to study the hawks and learn about their sounds and movements.[16] In this least realistic of plays Itow attempted a realistic imitation of the hawks which he had observed hopping about and stretching their wings.

Even Maire O'Neill's performance as Synge's Deirdre, which inspired Yeats to one of his best known pronouncements about the lack of character and the supreme importance of passion in tragedy (E and I 239–41), made him realize the importance of ordinary character development. When *Deirdre of the Sorrows* opened, Yeats confided to his journal his paradoxical sense that a feeling for the ordinary circumstances and emotions of life may be necessary to the expression of tragic passion:

> The chief failure is at the end. She does not show immediately after the death of Naisi enough sense of what has happened, enough *normal despair* to show a gradual development into the wild unearthly feeling of the last speeches, though these last speeches are in themselves exquisitely spoken. (MEM 240, my italics)

Yeats may have come to understand from Maire O'Neill's acting that without attention to normal circumstance and emotion, the expression of tragic passion would exist in a void.

Yeats loathed not so much the depiction of ordinary observed life as the habits and conventions of an outworn theatricalism that grew increasingly divorced from the expression of normal emotion. Indeed, it is instructive to note that Yeats and Stanislavsky, whose theaters were opposites in so many ways, would have agreed on this important point. Like Yeats, Stanislavsky hated the physical expression of feeling imposed by habit and divorced from the emotion it was expressing.[17] But Yeats was led by his own inclinations, as well as by the nature of his talent, away from observation and toward inner experience. Though he had exalted in his 1910 lectures on personality the sincere expression of felt emotion, as in a letter to a friend, he was always hard put to communicate the circumstances and details that might lead to the expression of that emotion. A remark he had made of Spenser applies with equal validity to much in his Abbey plays. "Perhaps to no European poet before his day had . . . the clear vision of the lineaments of human character [been] so difficult" (E and I 358). His own early plays were too often cut off from the life out of which they had to grow.

As Yeats committed himself to personal utterance in lyric poetry, he came to realize the need to create a personality to whom poetic utterance was possible—indeed, for whom poetic utterance was the natural and inevitable form of expression. He recorded early in his journal a description of the sort of personality necessary to his lyric poetry:

> this personality, (alas, to me only possible in my writings) must be always gracious and simple. It must have that slight separation from immediate interests which makes charm possible, while remaining near enough for fire. (MEM 142)

The creation of such personality was as necessary to Yeats's plays as to his lyric poetry. In his dramatic writing, he rarely had trouble maintaining the slight separation from life which "makes charm possible." But the personalities in his plays, even after many revisions, rarely came near enough to life for fire.

The Countess Cathleen first performed 1899; principal revisions 1911

A notable example of such over-separation from life can be found in *The Countess Cathleen*. This play depicts a cultured, wealthy landowner who sells her soul for a great price so that she may buy food for her starving tenants. As was the case with *Cathleen ni Houlihan,* Maud Gonne was a party to the birth of this play. Yeats recalled in the first draft of his autobiography that she had inspired the play, and he described the young Maud Gonne as seeking "some memorable action for final consecration of her youth" (MEM 42). The Countess of the play's first two scenes similarly seeks and finds such an action. But where Cathleen ni Houlihan, first acted by Maud Gonne, seems like her prototype a being fused and unified, the Countess even after sundry revisions suggests in her first two scenes a vague passivity. She acquires her passionate purpose, to succor the starving peasants and to sacrifice herself for them, only at the conclusion of the play's second scene.

> Come follow me, for the earth burns my feet,
> Till I have changed my house to such a refuge,
> That the old and ailing, and all weak of heart
> May escape from beak and claw. All, all shall come
> Till the walls burst and the roof fall on us.
> From this day out, I have nothing of my own.
>
> (CPL 15)

Una, her nurse and confidante, alerts the poet Aleel and the audience to the sea change in Cathleen's soul.

> She has found something now to put her hand to,
> And you and I are of no more account
> Than flies upon a windowpane in the winter.
>
> (CPL 16)

But the audience has been given no clear idea as to who exactly has been seized by this passionate purpose. When the Countess first comes on to the stage near the play's beginning, she wanders into Shemus Rua's cottage. The juxtaposition of the aristocrat and her entourage makes for a piece of effective theater, but the portrayal of Cathleen herself is vulnerable to strictures like those of Adrian Frazier.[18] Before she discovers her driving purpose, Cathleen is as inactive a tragic figure as can well be imagined. Her reasons for seeking her childhood home are stated with an indefiniteness and lack of urgency that the mature Yeats would not have tolerated. The author of Cathleen's early scenes, through all their revisions, is once again departing from Aristotle to the detriment of his play.

Character is that which reveals moral purpose, showing what kind of things a man chooses or avoids. Speeches, therefore, which do not make this manifest, or in which the speaker does not choose or avoid anything whatever, are not expressive of character.[19]

According to Aristotle's criteria, Cathleen's speeches are not expressive of character until her tragedy is half over.

Even after she discovers her moral purpose, she tends to act by proxy. She spends much of the play waiting in her offertory while her agents are busy on her errands. Her only direct action is to sell her soul, and even that action consists simply of signing a document, and then sinking into death. For Adrian Frazier, severe in his criticism of this play, she is representative of the idle, wealthy ascendancy, indulging her vague, cultured loneliness while her tenants starve.[20] This view is not entirely accurate—after all, she does attempt to sell all she has so that she may redress her peasants' plight. But Frazier is correct in pointing out how little this tragic figure is given to do. Indeed, while this may not be the dramatist's intention, Yeats manages to emphasize his chief figure's relative passivity by contrast to the other character's constant action. Aleel threatens the surly Shemus Rua with physical violence for insulting Cathleen, snaps his fingers under the peasant's nose, and receives a wound while running one of the countess's errands. Shemus beats his wife, conjures the demons, and puts himself forward as their chief agent in the merchandising of souls. Even Oona, while she speaks of Cathleen's newly acquired purpose, is bandaging Aleel's wounded hand. The play's final acting version possesses many theatrical virtues, but the portrayal of its principal personality is vitiated by a relative lack of definition in the early scenes, and by a relative inactivity throughout.

The Shadowy Waters first performed 1904; principal revisions 1905-6; 1911

As with everything else in Yeats's art, the expression of passionate personality on the stage was hard-won, achieved through years of never-ceasing toil. Much of this toil during Yeats's dramatic apprenticeship was lavished on revisions of *The Shadowy Waters*. He wrote to Arthur Symons after one such period of revision:

> The error of late periods like this is to believe that some things are inherently poetical, and to try and pull them on to the scene at every moment. It is just these seeming inherently poetical things that wear out. My *Shadowy Waters* was full of them, and the fundamental thinking was nothing, and that gave the whole poem an impression of weakness. There was no internal life pressing for expression through the characters. (L 460)

Even in its final acting version, internal life does not press so urgently as it does in Yeats's later plays. Set on board ship, this dramatic fantasy depicts Forgael, the aristocratic and reluctant captain of a pirate band, who is seeking a perfect love beyond the world's end. His greatest treasure is a magic harp with which he is able to charm all other human creatures into doing his will. The play's theme, the quest for something beyond the living world, mitigates against the creation of a character who is near enough to life for fire. Since Forgael is in fact sailing toward the secret place beyond life that all tragic figures must touch in metaphor, it is necessarily difficult for the dramatist to use life's circumstances in giving his character even minimal definition.

Finding a desperate Queen Dectora in strange seas, Forgael allays her fury with his magic harp. Dectora does not immediately relinquish her rage. Raising a weapon, perhaps to turn it either on him or on herself, she declares: "I will end all your magic on the instant" (CPL 104). But then, as he continues to play, her voice becomes dreamy, and she lowers the sword slowly and finally lets it fall. Lost in a dream induced by the harp, Dectora forgets her rage and falls in love with him. Having achieved his object, Forgael can now sail beyond life in quest of ecstasy.

But as Dectora's passion grows, Forgael suffers an agony of remorse because he has deceived her through illusion and supernatural agency. In a startling reversal of roles, Dectora tries to dissuade Forgael from his remorse with the strength of her newly awakened passion. The play's most compelling sequence occurs when Forgael momentarily pauses to consider what he is doing to Dectora.

> **FORGAEL** But I have done so great a wrong against you,
> There is no measure that it would not burst.
> I will confess it all.
> **DECTORA** What do I care?
> Now that my body has begun to dream

> And you have grown to be a burning coal
> In the imagination and intellect?
> . . . .
> Why do you weep?
> **FORGAEL**   I weep because I have nothing for your eyes
> But desolate waters and a battered ship.
>
> (CPL 107)

The reality of Forgael's deception presses upon his dream of a perfect love, and the internal conflict dramatically strengthens these lines. But for the most part, Forgael's dream of passion, separated from reality, does not sustain the force of a tragic personality. Most of the good lines are not spoken by the putative hero, but by his antagonists.

The play Yeats worked on for so long is emblematic both of his lofty goals for the theater and, paradoxically, that which most impeded him in his attempt to depict passionate personality. Like his creature Forgael, the poet was seeking beauty and ecstasy beyond life. But at the same time, the playwright was discovering, almost in spite of himself, that the circumstantial art of comedy heightens tragedy. Yeats had criticized Ibsen for depending on "little minute effects"[21] and forcing his audience to infer from such effects a passion that his characters could never fully express. Yeats's problem was opposite to Ibsen's. He had to give his persons sufficient definition in their normal moments that the spectators would be willing to mount with them to their supreme expressions of ecstasy.

Symptomatic of the problem is the relative inactivity of Yeats's early tragic protagonists. Despite his pronouncement that "A play must use or seem to use the bodily energies of its principal actor to the full" (E and I 245), his own early figures hardly exist physically. I have noted how little the Countess Cathleen has to do. Seanchan spends most of his play supine on the king's steps. Forgael is asleep at the beginning of his play. The action that leads to his apotheosis, namely the capturing of Dectora, is performed not by him but by his men. Like the Countess Cathleen, he waits while his servants do his will.

Only with the Cuchulain of *On Baile's Strand* and with Deirdre does Yeats create roles that require the sort of physically and emotionally exhausting performances he came so to admire. These are the most successful of his early tragedies, and what he learned about dramatic composition from writing and revising them is at least as important to his future development as his subsequent discovery of the Noh.

On Baile's Strand first performed 1904; revised 1906

Cuchulain is no otherworldly dreamer. His gusto, his appetite for the pleasures this world affords, is one of his defining characteristics. Through a series of tragic mistakes, this warrior hero unknowingly kills his own son in single combat. The spectators' sense of his terrible loss at the play's end is heightened by his continuing adherence to normal emotions and desires, chief among them the desire for a son and worthy heir.

This is the first of Yeats's tragic roles to demand such bodily exertion of its performer as the playwright later came to insist upon. Padraic Colum tells an instructive story of Frank Fay in the part.

> Now Frank Fay was far from heroic in his build, but he could project himself as an heroic figure, as he did not have to draw the audience's attention to his bodily equipment. But he had to take hold of the arm of the young man who was his son and ejaculate: "That arm had a good father and a good mother / But it is not like this!" and strip his own to show an arm as meagre as any townsman's. It was wonderful that he could do it and leave only a momentary sense of incongruity.[22]

The story is instructive of a truth, too often forgotten by theater people who should know better, that a performer's physical appearance is less important than the ability emotionally and intellectually to project a role. Colum's anecdote is equally important because Cuchulain is the first of Yeats's major theatrical figures about whom such a story could be told, since Cuchulain's passion must be expressed physically, as well as with mind and spirit.

That Cuchulain is both more complex and more substantial than Yeats's other early stage figures is suggested by the playwright's correspondence with Frank Fay about the role. Yeats offered the actor a surprisingly Stanislavskian analysis of Cuchulain's psychology and history. The Cuchulain of legend

> never ages. I have to recognize that he does, for he has a son who is old enough to fight him. I have also to make the refusal of the son's affection tragic by suggesting in Cuchulain's character a shadow of

1 / THE PROBLEM OF PERSONALITY

> something a little proud, barren and restless, as if out of sheer strength of heart or from accident he had put affection away. He lives among young men but has himself outlived the illusions of youth. He is probably about forty, not less than thirty-five or thirty-six and not more than forty-five or forty-six, certainly not an old man, and one understands from his talk about women that he does not love like a young man.... He is a little hard, and leaves the people about him a little repelled—perhaps this young man's affection is what he had most need of. (L 424–25)

Cuchulain is the first of his creator's major tragic figures who admits of such circumstantial analysis, and who is yet capable of the lyric expression of personality.

This protagonist fits Yeats's definition of tragedy: "passion defined by motives."[23] His motives are mixed, and they undergo several radical changes during the course of the action. In this respect also he differs from his counterparts in the other early plays. For the most part, the figures in these plays are all in single-minded pursuit of a passionate purpose. They are not given to internal conflict of a sort to which Hamlet or Macbeth have accustomed readers and theater audiences, and they do not change their minds. Cuchulain, precisely unlike Yeats's other early dramatis personae, changes his mind with astonishing rapidity several times during this short play. Indeed, his tragedy turns on the wandering of his passion from motive to motive.

Cuchulain's first scene is a clash of wills with Conchubar. Behind his passion not to be bound to another man's will is the deeper, stronger passion of regret and remorse that he does not have a son worthy of him. He changes his mind about the oath Conchubar is trying to force on him when he realizes that the other young kings, his companions, are settling into a domesticity he both longs for and shuns.

> **A YOUNG KING**   Do what the high king bids you.
> **CONCHUBAR**   There is not one but dreads this turbulence
> Now that they're settled men.
> **CUCHULAIN**   Are you so changed?
> Or have I grown more dangerous of late?
> But that's not it. I understand it all.
> It's you that have changed. You've wives and children now,
> And for that reason cannot follow one
> That lives like a bird's flight from tree to tree.

> It's time the years put water in my blood
> And drowned the wildness of it, for all's changed;
> But that's unchanged. I'll take what oath you will.
> The moon, the sun, the water, light or air,
> I do not care how binding.
>
> (CPL 171)

Delivered with a sense of terrible disappointment, these lines can generate considerable tragic power. Cuchulain is allowing himself to be bound because he discovers that his freedom is no longer worth pursuing.

No sooner has he taken the oath than the young stranger enters with his challenge. Cuchulain befriends the young man, Conchubar forbids it, and Cuchulain strikes the high king. His subsequent lines will be most effective when spoken quietly, with a growing horror. Only some terrible enchantment could have induced Cuchulain to this unthinkable, treasonous act.

> **FIRST OLD KING** Some witch has worked upon your mind, Cuchulain.
> The head of that young man seemed like a woman's
> You'd had a fancy for. Then of a sudden
> You laid your hands on the high king himself!
> **CUCHULAIN** And laid my hands on the high king himself?
> **CONCHUBAR** Some witch is floating in the air above us.
> **CUCHULAIN** Yes, witchcraft! Witchcraft! Witches of the air!
> (to young man) Why did you? who was it set you to this work?
> Out, out! I say, for now it's sword on sword!
>
> (CPL 177)

Far more than does Macbeth, Cuchulain outruns the pauser, reason. This sequence anticipates the terrible moment when, in reaction to the chatter of the fool and the blind man, Cuchulain divines the identity of the young man he has killed. When he gets his first intimation of the truth, his horror is so great he is unable to speak. His passion is expressed wholly in action. The fool tells him that the blind man had

> said a while ago that he heard Aoife's boast that she'd never but the one lover, and he the only man that had overcome her in battle. (pause)
> **BLIND MAN** Somebody is trembling fool. The bench is shaking.

Why are you trembling? Is Cuchulain going to hurt us? It was not I who told you, Cuchulain.
FOOL   It is Cuchulain who is trembling. It is Cuchulain who is shaking the bench.
BLIND MAN   It is his own son he has slain.

(CPL 180)

Yeats's inchoate theory merges with his practice in this difficult moment. The actor playing Cuchulain, without speaking a word, must express the force of the fighting man's grief and rage with every lineament of his unified being. Once again a figure in a Yeats play illustrates one of Lukacs's conclusions about personality. "Man grows dramatic by virtue of the intensity of his will, by the outpouring of its essence in his deeds."[24] Cuchulain pours his entire being into his sudden act of violence. Seizing on the idea that Conchubar is the root cause of his loss, he again rushes out with the cry: "Conchubar! Conchubar! This sword into your heart!" (CPL 181)

The fool points to the fundamental enmity between Cuchulain and the high king when he describes the fight with the sea:

He sees king Conchubar's crown in every one of them! . . . He has killed kings and giants, but the waves have mastered him! The waves have mastered him! (CPL 181)

In creating this frenzied, violent, rushing hero, Yeats departs significantly from Lady Gregory's retelling of this tale in *Cuchulain of Muirthemne*, and from his own earlier verse narrative, first published in the *Countess Cathleen* volume in 1892. In these versions Conchubar, aided by Druid magic, manipulates Cuchulain into fighting the waves, in order to keep the raging hero from killing the high king.

> Then Conchubar, the subtlest of all men,
> Ranking his Druids round him ten by ten,
> Spake thus: "Cuchulain will dwell there and brood
> For three days more in dreadful quietude,
> And then arise, and raving slay us all.
> Chaunt in his ear delusions magical,
> That he may fight the horses of the sea."
> The Druids took them to their mystery,
> And chaunted for three days. Cuchulain stirred,

> Stared on the horses of the sea, and heard
> The cars of battle and his own name cried;
> And fought with the invulnerable tide. (CP 41)

Yeats had made similar use of magical agency in *The Shadowy Waters*, and in that play's various revisions, Forgael's harp and the supernatural birds remain primary causes of the action. The fact that Yeats in *On Baile's Strand* departed both from the received legend and from his own previous handling of the tale suggests that he was beginning to perceive that supernatural agency, as a sole motivating force, can be incompatible with the highest tragedy. He was to continue to use the supernatural in many subsequent plays. But like Sophocles and Shakespeare, and significantly unlike the creators of the Noh plays, he fashioned tragic figures for whom the ghosts or shadows, the unappeasable mountain witches, constitute only a single strand of the web within which they must express passion through action. From the Cuchulain of this play on, Yeats's tragic figures, though often opposed by ghosts or magical forces, do not commit the actions that define their tragedies while under some spell. Even the Cuchulain of *At the Hawk's Well* acts independently at the last.

The Cuchulain of *On Baile's Strand*, unlike the Cuchulain of the earlier poem or of the legend, is not driven to his deeds by witches, for all his talk of witches. The forces in his own nature find their fullest and inevitable expression in his offer of friendship to the young man, in his sudden fury against that same young man, and in his final frenzy of rage and grief that begins in his silent trembling and ends in his fighting the sea. This is the first of Yeats's tragic figures to find deeds that adequately express his passion, and those deeds use to the full the actor's bodily energies. When Cuchulain does speak in the height of his passion, the full force of his life is pressing for expression through his lines.

To be sure, it is possible to find fault with Cuchulain. The criticisms of Strong and Ellmann apply to him, as they do to figures in Yeats's other pre-Noh plays. The audience never finds Cuchulain in the act of passionate hesitation, or of coming to terms with his own nature. Tragedy grows out of the horror accompanying Cuchulain's recognition that he has killed his son. But Cuchulain never comes to that full, tragic knowledge of himself to which the Greek tragedians, Shakespeare, and Racine have accustomed generations of audiences and readers. He strikes out at those whom he holds to blame—the witches, the young man, Conchubar, the waves—but he never comes to share his creator's recognition that his chief nemesis is himself. Thus, though *On Baile's Strand* in its revised version is a stirring piece of poetic drama, and constitutes a breakthrough in Yeats's composition for the stage at least as important as *At the Hawk's Well*, the characteristics I have been describing prevent audiences and readers from receiving the full measure of tragic catharsis from the play.

Such characteristics remain with Yeats throughout his career as a playwright. He admired Hamlet's passionate hesitations, recognizing the lines that spring from them as among the great achievements in poetic drama. But in Yeats's own plays, early and late, impulse is translated to action on the instant. His dramatis personae do not, as a rule, exhibit the doubt and vacillation from which arises much of the power in his lyric poetry. Rare indeed are such moments of doubt as Forgael exhibits, and Yeats's dramatic *oeuvre*, for all its strengths, is weakened by this rarity.

Deirdre first performed 1906; revised 1908

With *On Baile's Strand*, *Deirdre* in its revised form constitutes the pinnacle of Yeats's pre-Noh tragic achievement. A dramatization of Ireland's best-known legend, the play depicts the last terrible hours of Deirdre and her lover Naoise. Deirdre, having fled with her lover from the old King Conchubar to whom she had been betrothed, returns with Naoise after years of exile to a final betrayal. The old king has Naoise killed, and Deirdre kills herself upon her lover's body.

Yeats came to believe that he had written a great play, and he took pride in the play's grip upon the audience. He also recognized, as he prepared the play for production, that it would require a performer of genius. He thought he had found such a performer in the actress Florence Darragh, and some of his worst quarrels with his fellow directors Synge and Lady Gregory were precipitated by his insistence that she become the company's new leading lady for tragic parts. Synge and Gregory never thought that Darragh was up to the role. Indeed, Synge found her performance characterized by those very theatrical habits and conventions that Yeats was to indict in his remarks on the commercial theater.

> I greatly dislike the impression that Deirdre or rather Miss Darragh has left on me. Emotion, if it cannot be given with some trace of distinction or nobility, is best left to the imagination of the audience.[25]

In a subsequent letter to Yeats, Lady Gregory expressed her own disapprobation of Darragh:

> You couple with the great name of passion, on which we should fight together, the name of an actress who I never heard objected to because she put passion in her parts, but because she put something mean, ignoble and sensual.[26]

In the event, Yeats himself grew dissatisfied with Darragh's performance, and it was not until Mrs. Patrick Campbell played Deirdre in 1908 that he got a performance that completely satisfied him.

Yet his initial obsession with Darragh's performance and his subsequent disappointment suggest an uncertainty about the play. Yeats had a clear idea that he needed a special kind of acting for the play, and he knew that he was not getting what he wanted from the performers regularly available to him at the Abbey. Even Frank Fay was beginning to disappoint him.[27]

Yeats believed that Darragh had the proper quality of intellectual tragedy for *Deirdre*, and he wrote exultantly to his father about her in July, 1906.

> She gave a magnificent performance of *Salome* the other day. I am inclined to think, though I have not seen enough of her yet to be quite certain, that she is the finest tragedian on the English stage. I feel that a change is taking place in the nature of acting; Mrs. Campbell and her generation were trained in plays like *Mrs. Tanqueray*, where everything is done by a kind of magnificent hysteria (one understands that when one hears her hunting her monkey and her servant with an impartial fury about the house). This school reduces everything to an emotional least common denominator. It finds the scullion in the queen, because there are scullions in the audience but no queens. (L 475–76)

Mrs. Patrick Campbell emerges as the *bête noire* in this letter. Yet it was she who was to triumph in *Deirdre* the following year. It may be that her very abilities as a conventional character actress, disparaged by Yeats as "magnificent hysteria," anchored her performance in his

1 / THE PROBLEM OF PERSONALITY

tragedy. The actress's attention to the very details of normal emotion that the playwright tended to gloss over may have contributed to their joint triumph with *Deirdre*.

Not everyone liked Mrs. Pat in the part. Padraic Colum wrote that she

> insisted upon playing Deirdre almost as she might play Magda, and she loses something of the tragic dignity; nor was that all. There was no limelight. But such an actress can drag the eye where she chooses. And at one critical moment where attention should center upon Naoise's first recognition of an evil omen, we were watching by-play between her and the singing girls.[28]

Despite such strictures, Stella Campbell's Deirdre became one of the few performances that entirely satisfied the playwright. Her conventional abilities as a character actress, combined with her ability to steal focus at need, may have paradoxically elevated her to Yeats's personal pantheon. Her performance was perhaps emblematic of the fusion of character with personality in his best plays.

Yeats knew that the actress playing Deirdre would have to achieve red heat before Naoise is murdered, white heat afterward. After Naoise's death, language and action are fused in that white heat into an expression of the highest passion. Ellis-Fermor's description remains, after more than fifty years, apt and accurate. She writes that Deirdre's last moments have "the authentic note of grim tragic action, word and deed following too swiftly for more than brief and memorable comment. It is a universalising of the old story, a realising of it again in terms of all human experience."[29] She adds that the play is distinguished by

> an immediacy as terrible as that of Middleton, severest of Jacobean tragic poets; and it has been achieved, as the Jacobean and the Greek dramatists achieved it, not by the quenching, but by the exultation of the poetic imagination.[30]

An indication both of the play's greatness and of its uncertainties can be gathered from Yeats's assessment of Mrs. Patrick Campbell's performance, which he described in "On the Boiler" as "passionate and solitary" (EXP 416). Deirdre is indeed solitary during the play's final moments, facing the terrible isolation consequent to Naoise's murder. The play is at its strongest in such moments, but at its weakest in her scenes with her lover. Although hers is one of the world's great love tragedies, her relations with Naoise are rather postulated than developed.

> **DEIRDRE**   And yet I think
> That being half-good I might change round again
> Were we aboard our ship and on the sea.
> **NAOISE**   We'll to the horses and take ship again.
> **FERGUS**   Fool, she but seeks to rouse your jealousy
> With crafty words.
>
> (CPL 122)

Padraic Colum offers a dry assessment of this exchange. "Naoise has been Deirdre's husband for nine years; he would know, of course, that what she was saying was not true; she would know that he would know it, and so would not say anything of the kind."[31] The passage suggests Yeats's impatience with the circumstances whose depiction the dramatic form required. The playwright's Wildean boredom with and contempt for the vulgar details that lead to the moments of solitary passion tend to vitiate the effect of some of the greatest tragic verse of our century.

Such deceit and irritation as the scenes between Naoise and Deirdre suggest can credibly become parts of erotic tragedy. *Antony and Cleopatra* is full of such sequences, and Cleopatra's final scenes with Caesar, leading to the solitary passion of her death, are similar in form, as well as in dramatic and poetic power, to the final moments of *Deirdre*. But Shakespeare dramatically develops the complex interplay among amorous passion, deceit, irritation, and anger. Yeats merely asserts them. The play does not take fire until the lovers realize that their only way out is through death. From that point on, the dramatist's attention seems fully engaged, and the play achieves the power for which Ellis-Fermor celebrates it.

Yeats might have corrected against the shortcomings in the play's first half had he taken a path similar to that taken, two or three years later, by Synge in his Deirdre play. In some respects, Synge's task was easier than Yeats's. As Lennox Robinson points out, the story of Deirdre falls naturally into three acts. Robinson argues that Yeats, in choosing to make a one-act play of that story, set for himself a far harder task.[32] In the greater space afforded him by the three-act

1 / THE PROBLEM OF PERSONALITY

form, Synge was able, as Yeats was not, to develop the growth and decay of the lovers' passion.

Yeats admired no play more than Synge's *Deirdre of the Sorrows*, and in one of the 1910 lectures on personality he described Synge's achievement. Yeats's precise analysis of Synge's circumstantial dramaturgy stands as an indictment of his own. He pointed out that Deirdre, in Synge, feels that certain death "is better than for her love for Naisi gradually to dwindle away with age."[33] In Synge's play, as Yeats describes it, the lovers are depicted in the act of growing weary of each other, and Naisi's increasing irritation with his years in exile is revealed by the dialogue.[34] Through a dramatic development of these themes, Synge achieves a circumstantial credibility and consistency lacking in Yeats's play. Through an extended analysis of Synge's achievement, Yeats concedes, in the midst of one of his central documents on personality, the necessity for conventional character development in tragedy.

Such feelings as are revealed in Synge's Naisi might be inferred in Yeats's Naoise, but the dramatist does not develop them. The spectators gather a sense of amorous passion only after it becomes clear to the man that he is to die. Kneeling at his feet, Deirdre utters one of the play's most passionate and memorable speeches. Her lines are all the more compelling in that they constitute, relatively late in the play, the first extended development the spectators have yet heard of this tragedy's amorous theme.

> Do you remember that first night in the woods?
> We lay all night on leaves, and looking up,
> When the first grey of the dawn awoke the birds,
> Saw leaves above us? You thought that I still slept.
> And bending down to kiss me on the eyes,
> Found they were open. Bend and kiss me now.
> For it may be the last before our death,
> And when that's over, we'll be different;
> Imperishable things, a cloud or a fire;
> And I know nothing but this body: nothing
> But that old vehement bewildering kiss.
>
> (CPL 126)

This speech does not lead, as it might have in *Romeo and Juliet* or *Antony and Cleopatra* to a duet in which Eros and Thanatos combine.

Conchubar's appearance distracts Naoise, who rushes out Cuchulain-like to fall into the high king's trap.

His capture and murder occasion the best writing in the play. In her scenes with Conchubar, Deirdre passes from the normal pathos of pleading vainly for her lover's life to the calm of absolute decision when she perceives that she must join him in death.

> O do not touch me! Let me go to him!
> (pause)
> King Conchubar is right. My husband's dead.
> A single woman is of no account,
> Lacking array of servants, linen cupboards,
> The bacon hanging, and King Conchubar's house
> All ready too.
>   (CPL 131)

The tragedy turns upon the pause. In that moment, Deirdre passes from red heat to white heat. There is no more need for the outward flourishes of rage, the screams and the violent gestures. Now her entire being, fused, unified, and possessed of a calm, terrifying intensity, is bent on one purpose alone: to fool Conchubar into allowing her the few moments she will require to join Naoise in death. She has passed to the secret place beyond life, and Yeats finds action and language that afford the complete expression of her whole nature.

> Now strike the wire and sing to it awhile;
> Knowing that all is happy, and that you know
> Within what bridebed I shall lie this night;
> And by what man: and lie close up to him—
> For the bed's narrow— and there out-sleep the cock-crow.
>   (CPL 133)

In this speech, rhythmically compelling, full of detail that is both dramatic and sensuous, beauty of line is inseparable from power of situation. But actors and audiences alike must negotiate some difficult passages in this play in order to arrive at this point of beauty and power. Paradoxically, Yeats gave too much attention to what he would call the "wheels and pulleys" (E and I 238) the conventional mechanisms of plot and character, for readers and spectators to overlook them. The play's awkward moments come about because the dramatist chafed at having to depict such "rhetoric and logic and dry circumstance" (VPL 391) that credibly precede the emotional state he wanted to communicate. The new form of drama based on the Noh which he was to invent would permit him to enter the lives of his plays' characters at the precise point at which they were achieving the states of soul that most interested him. Their means of arriving at those states of soul could be suggested indirectly and lyrically, rather than through the direct, dry logic of dramatic dialogue. In the later plays, he was able to avoid the gradual opening out of events and proceed directly to the "blue heart of the flame."[35] Equally important, he was able to pay just enough attention to the ordinary lives and emotions of his characters to make his audiences care about their passions.

Yeats had argued in "The Tragic Theatre" that character grew less in the great ages of tragedy (E and I 240), and it is a critical commonplace that character grew less in his own plays from *At the Hawk's Well* onward. What is not so generally recognized is that he never abandoned the principle that a certain amount of ordinary detail and normal emotion must anchor the story, even though its persons are moving toward the secret place beyond life. Even the Guardian of the Well, as remote a figure as Yeats ever conceived, is informed by the substance of a real hawk at the London Zoo. Thus, Yeats made sure to include just enough telling detail in his mature plays to catch and hold his spectators' passionate attention. He knew that too much detail and circumstance could vitiate his plays' lyricism, but he was also discovering that too little detail could so divorce his plays from life that no spectators, however poetically cultivated, would give their sympathy or interest.

At the Hawk's Well first performed 1916

In this first of Yeats's plays for dancers, an old man and a young man, both seeking the waters of immortality, keep watch by a dry well. In early drafts of the play, the young man identifies himself as Cuchulain, and the old man, recognizing the name, simply recounts Cuchulain's known reputation.

> **YOUNG MAN**   I am named Cuchulain. I am Sualtim's son.
> I have an ancient house beyond the sea.

> **OLD MAN**   I have heard that name about a shepherd's fire.
> What mischief brings you hither? For they say
> That you are crazy to shed blood of men
> And crazy after women.[36]

In later drafts, and in the play's final form, the passage has evolved into a moment of fine dramatic irony, a piece of revelation of character through action that sets Cuchulain clearly before the spectators, and captures their interest in this peculiar personality.

> **YOUNG MAN**   I am Cuchulain. I am Sualtim's son.
> **OLD MAN**   I have never heard that name.
> **YOUNG MAN**   It is not unknown.
> I have an ancient house beyond the sea.
> **OLD MAN**   What mischief brings you hither? You are like those
> Who are crazy for the shedding of men's blood
> And for the love of women.
>
> (CPL 139)

The playwright inserts a sardonic joke into this strange play. Cuchulain is punctured at not being recognized. His vanity is piqued, yet his pride will not allow him to boast to a stranger. The old man can draw conclusions about bloodshed and women from his appearance and manner, rather than simply reciting the facts of a known reputation which the play's action has not earned. With this apparently small alteration, Yeats gives spectators and readers ironic insight into the personalities of both figures. The seemingly insignificant detail anchors the play in life.

A similarly revealing moment occurs when the old man tells the young one that the Sidhe may cast a magic sleep upon him just as the waters fill the well.

> **YOUNG MAN**   My luck is strong.
> It will not leave me waiting, nor will they
> That dance among the stones put me asleep.
> If I grow drowsy, I can pierce my foot.
> **OLD MAN**   No! Do not pierce it, for the foot is tender.
> It feels pain much.
>
> (CPL 140)

This contrast between the overbold young man and the overcautious old man is revealed by a brief, circumstantial sequence of dramatic irony. In performance, the moment may even get a smile from the audience.

A short play whose chief aim is to communicate states of the soul needs only a few such minute particulars of ordinary life and normal emotion. None of these particulars gives the play its greatness or its eerie strangeness. But that separating strangeness would divorce the work entirely from all spectators had not the dramatist taken the trouble to incorporate details and circumstances such as these. Without them, the play would be the artistic novelty, neither theater nor poetry, that Sean O'Casey has accused it of being.[37] With them, the play is just substantial enough to hold its audience's attention, and to endure.

The Only Jealousy of Emer completed 1919; performed 1926

Similar minute particulars, tiny moments of circumstantial irony that give insight into the personalities of the figures on the stage, can be found in Yeats's subsequent plays. There are never many of these, but there are always just enough. In *The Only Jealousy of Emer*, as in the much earlier *The Shadowy Waters*, a supernatural agency persuades a strong-minded woman to change her mind. But where in the earlier play the raging Dectora is simply hypnotized into falling in love with Forgael by the magic harp, Emer in the later play agrees to renounce Cuchulain forever because of a circumstance of character in action that the playwright has precisely chosen and precisely applied. The play depicts Emer, wife of the amorous, violent Cuchulain, cherishing the hope that her faithless husband will at last return to her. Cuchulain, hovering in stasis between life and death, is wooed by one of the Sidhe, the amoral creatures who, in Irish legend, come from under the sea to disturb human affairs. Only if Emer renounces Cuchulain's love forever will he be released from an eternal amour with a non-human mistress.

Readers or rarer spectators of the play will recall that Emer, through Bricriu's malevolent power, is able to perceive Fand in the act of wooing her husband's shade. The vision consists of a stylized dance and a dialogue in tetrameter couplets. The scene embodies all that separating strangeness for which Yeats was striving in these plays. Yet in the midst of this most unearthly of wooings, the spectators encounter a detail of ordinary domestic life.

GHOST OF CUCHULAIN   Your mouth!
(They are about to kiss. He turns away.)
Oh Emer! Emer!
WOMAN OF THE SIDHE   So then it is she
Made you impure with memory.
GHOST OF CUCHULAIN   Oh Emer! Emer! There we stand
Side by side and hand in hand,
Tread the threshold of the house
As when our parents married us.
WOMAN OF THE SIDHE   Being among the dead, you love her,
That valued every slut above her
While you still lived.
GHOST OF CUCHULAIN   Oh my lost Emer!

(CPL 192)

Entering upon an act of supernatural adultery, the husband experiences a pang of natural remorse as he recalls his wife. Cuchulain turns "from a statue / His too human breast," (CPL 193) and Emer renounces his love forever. The climax of this, possibly the greatest and certainly the strangest of Yeats's dance plays, is brought about by the depiction of an ordinary domestic detail, a would-be adulterer's remorse, that would not have been out of place in a play by Ibsen or Shaw.

The author of *Four Plays for Dancers*, *A Full Moon in March*, and *Purgatory* is as great a master of poetic drama as the author of *The Tower* and *The Winding Stair* is of lyric poetry. In inventing a form which frees the playwright from an excess of dry circumstance, Yeats paradoxically freed himself to make use of just the right amount of circumstance, neither too little nor too much. His selection of such circumstance was marked by just such passion and precision as was his selection of the poem's proper word. The man who had shunned dry circumstance in his early plays, fearing that it would spoil his poetic faculty and make his mind arid and abstract, did not refrain from embracing "fat greasy life" in *Purgatory*. In *The Words Upon the Window Pane*, the separating strangeness of the medium allowed Yeats to do what he could not do in *Deirdre*: namely to create an erotic scene in which amorous passion mingles with hatred, contempt, and pain. Bent in his later plays on the fashioning of passionate personalities, Yeats fused into those personalities sufficient circumstantial detail to create examples of enduring life. However strange that life, it remains human.

2
Writing for the Ear

I have spent my life clearing out of poetry every phrase written for the eye, and bringing all back to syntax that is for ear alone. Write for the ear, I thought, so that you may be instantly understood, as when actor or folk singer stands before an audience.

—*"An Introduction to my Plays"*

In the plays for dancers, and in some of the plays that followed them, Yeats created what is arguably the first fully successful poetic drama in English since the seventeenth century. An observation by Edmund Wilson about Yeats's lyric verse applies to the plays he wrote from 1916 onward.

> His words, no matter how prosaic, are always somehow luminous and noble, as if pale pebbles smoothed by the sea were to take on some mysterious value and become more precious than jewels or gold.[1]

Maud Gonne, to whom many of Yeats's most memorable words are addressed, wrote a letter to him after receiving one of his books that describes his verse in similar terms.

> What makes the extraordinary charm of your poetry is the terrible though unseen effort of its creation. This somehow makes the atmosphere of a precious jewel about it. Like a gem, it is the outcome of a terrible and hidden effort.[2]

Examination of successive plays in their various drafts reveals his unremitting effort to find words, sounds, rhythms, and syntax that give his hearers the continuous impression of a living speaker. The words in his plays gain nobility and value from their rhythmic relations to each other, from their placement within the metric patterns

Yeats employs, from their sound, and from the powerful passionate syntax the playwright always sought (E and I 521).

Yeats composed for the voice *and* the ear. His failing eyesight heightened his natural inclination to restore words to their ancient sovereignty in the theater, and to subordinate to them the theater's other resources. When composing he spoke his words aloud, and he heard them spoken, often with distinction, by many performers. No writer of the twentieth century has given more attention to the speaker and the listener. My own lack of eyesight, coupled with the fact that I, like Yeats, spend many professional hours listening to spoken verse, to adjusting in rehearsal its pace, pitch, and rhythm, to helping speakers understand and communicate its passionate syntax, may enable me to speak with some authority on Yeats's use of the ancient Aristotelian elements of diction and song. While the blind have no monopoly in discussions of the ear and the voice, there may be something to be said for Yeats's position (E and I 530) that in matters of speaking and listening, the eye may be a distraction.

Any inquiry into Yeats's evolving mastery of drama must take into account the supreme importance he gave to words in the theater. His use of words in carefully crafted patterns of sound, rhythm, and syntax constitute a major source of his best plays' power. Diction and song were the only ancient elements of drama with which the playwright did not engage—as he did with character, plot, and thought—in lifelong conflict. From the beginning, he was a master of words in the theater; indeed, he can serve as illustration for one of Aristotle's shrewdest observations that "novices in the art attain to finish of diction and precision of portraiture before they can construct the plot."[3] Certainly it was not until Yeats began to master the plot that his early mastery of words in the theater achieved its full effect.

The alternation of stressed and unstressed syllables imposed by the metrical patterns Yeats usually used in his verse plays was balanced by the rhythmic variety he sought to create within that pattern. He compared the metrical pattern to the ticking of a watch. The imposition of rhythmic variety upon this metrical pattern results in "the ticking of the watch made softer that one must needs listen and various that one may not be swept beyond memory or grow weary of listening" (E and I 159). Much changed in Yeats's lyric and dramatic verse between the 1890s and the 1930s, but in a 1937 essay we find him holding firmly to the necessary relation between metrical pattern and the rhythmic variety that exists in counterpoint to that pattern. The pattern, Yeats continued to insist, gives stability and permanence to the personal utterance of lyric and dramatic verse. "All that is personal soon rots. It must be packed in ice or salt (E and I 522).

Adhering to his principle that "ancient salt is best packing" he almost always chose a traditional meter. Thus he composed many of his dramatic speeches in blank verse, the same form that had been used by Shakespeare and the other Elizabethan playwrights. This form carried with it a complex sense of history. "When I speak blank verse and analyze my feelings, I stand at a moment of history when instinct, its traditional songs and dances, its general agreement, is of the past" (E and I 524). But this sense of the past, conjured to the speaker's voice and the listener's ear by the metrical form of blank verse, had to be balanced by the immediacy and urgency of the present. Verse rhythms had to create a counterpoint in which past and present could be heard simultaneously. For Yeats, the ancient voice of the folk could still be heard in the rhythmic variety of dramatic verse dialogue.

> The folk song is still there, but a ghostly voice, an invariable possibility, an unconscious norm. What moves me and my hearer is a vivid speech that has no laws except that it must not exorcise the ghostly voice. (E and I 524)

The Only Jealousy of Emer completed 1919; performed 1926

Continuous counterpoint between living speech and ghostly voice gives the speeches in *The Only Jealousy of Emer* much of their power. Near the play's beginning, the audience sees the masked, motionless figure of Cuchulain lying on a bed, and hears the following blank verse dialogue between Emer, his wife, and Eithne Inguba, his mistress.

> **EMER** Come hither. Come sit down beside the bed.
> You need not be afraid, for I myself
> Sent for you, Eithne Inguba.
> **EITHNE** No madam.
> I have too deeply wronged you to sit there.
> **EMER** Of all the people in the world, we two

> And we alone may watch together here,
> Because we have loved him best.
> **EITHNE** And is he dead?
>
> (CPL 185–86)

Blank verse imposes on those who write it a metrical pattern, or arithmetical norm, consisting of a fixed number of syllables in a fixed relation. The metrical pattern establishes a Platonic idea of the verse line, and that idea is heard, however distantly, in every rhythmic variation. Seemingly arbitrary relations among syllables remain appealing because they remind the listener of a long and rich past that subsumes nursery songs as well as Marlowe and Shakespeare.

Poetic power is achieved not from slavish adherence to a metrical pattern, but rather through controlled departure from it. Yeats finds many ways to depart from the pattern without breaking it. Sometimes he raises the emphasis on the unstressed syllable so that it matches, or nearly matches, the stressed syllable. The juxtaposition of two heavily stressed syllables forces the speaker to retard and places unusual weight on the phrase so stressed, as in the line,

> *Come hi*ther. *Come sit down* be*side* the *bed.*

The commonplace phrase, "sit down," derives a dirge-like slowness from its two strongly stressed syllables. The two words strike the ear with even greater force because they occur at the exact center of the blank verse line, and they follow the strongly stressed "come." Thus, three strongly stressed monosyllables guide the speaker to give the line the quality of a dead march. The words are prosaic, but they take on nobility and value from their rhythmic relation to each other, as well as to the metrical pattern against which they play. The lines' grammar enhances their metrical power. Emer is uttering two commands. Each of her sentences begins with the strongly stressed imperative verb.

Sometimes Yeats reverses the fixed order of the iambic foot so that the stressed syllable precedes the unstressed one instead of following it. He is particularly fond of such inversions when the word he stresses is a verb, and when it occurs either at the beginning of a line or immediately after a pronounced pause in the midst of a line. The inversion, placing a stress where the ear has become accustomed not to hear one, indicates that the speaker should put special emphasis on the word:

> You need not be afraid, for I myself
> *Sent* for you, Eithne Inguba.
>
> And thereupon, *know*ing what man he had killed.
>
> (CPL 186)

In the first of the quoted lines, a reflexive separates the subject from the verb. Yeats often separates his stressed verb either from its subject or its object. "I myself / *Sent*," "I have too deeply *wronged*." Such separation combines with the stress itself in imparting power to the verb. The second of the quoted lines contains yet another example of controlled departure from the metrical norm. This is the insertion of an extra unstressed syllable into the line, thereby creating a foot that contains three syllables, two unstressed and one stressed: "he had *killed*." The three-syllable foot gives the line a lilt, and it also guides the speaker to hurry over the extra unstressed syllable. In this case, the three-syllable foot follows two other feet, each of which is also departing from the metrical pattern. In addition to the inverted foot "knowing" there is "what man," a near spondee, that is, a foot whose two syllables are almost equally stressed. These deliberate departures invite the speaker to stress "knowing," to retard slightly on "what man," and to accelerate slightly on "he had killed." Rhythmic departures from the metrical pattern are likely to increase either when the speaker grows agitated, or when an important thought or event is being described.

Often in Yeats's dramatic dialogue, the end of a speech does not coincide with the end of a line. One speaker may conclude with a partial line, and the next speaker will begin by completing the line. Emer's "Sent for you, Eithne Inguba," finishes her thought and her sentence, but consists of only four of the five feet necessary to make up the blank verse line. Eithne Inguba's "No madam" responds to Emer and completes her line. This device can suggest a growing sympathy between speakers. The same device, used differently, can also suggest growing conflict between speakers. Often in Yeats's dramatic verse, sympathy and conflict exist simultaneously. For example, a line shared between two speakers occurs at the play's climax. The god of discord is urging Emer to make her renunciation or lose her husband to his immortal seducer.

> Renounce him, and her power is at an end.
> Cuchulain's foot is on the chariot-step.
> Cry———
> **EMER** I renounce Cuchulain's love for ever.
>
> (VPL 561)

Emer's renunciation completes Bricriu's line. Her nine syllables, joined to his "cry" create a single line. The apparently small detail of versification greatly heightens the climax, for it creates the sense that Emer at this moment is at one with the maker of discord who possesses her husband's body. Making her choice, she becomes simultaneously greater than herself and, at the same time, an extension of Bricriu's will. Her "I" coupled with his "Cry" creates spondee and assonance, bringing about a power and strangeness that could not be achieved in any other way.

Demanding as is verse drama to its writers and performers, it makes equal demands upon its audience. It presumes sustained attention, and a knowledge and love of language as a sensuous way of expressing deep feeling as well as complex and subtle thought. But Yeats knew as well as anyone that "the emotion that comes with the music of words is exhausting, like all intellectual emotions, and few people like exhausting emotions" (E and I 169). He knew that his ideal audience must have a traditional knowledge of poetry as well as an ear keen to subtle variations of cadence, rhythm, or substitutions from expected words, "And neither is possible without rich leisurely minds in the audience, lovers of Father Time, men who understand Faust's last cry to the passing moment" (MEM 210). He grew convinced that the large, heterogeneous audience, even at the Abbey, was losing its sense of and taste for poetry. Sound, rhythm, and metaphor were becoming ever less accessible to such an audience. This was one reason that Yeats invented a private, intimate, aristocratic form of drama.

Sophocles' *King Oedipus* first performed 1927

But as he demonstrated during the twenties and thirties, after the publication of his dance plays intended for private performance, he could employ a language as rich in imaginative suggestion as was the language of those plays, and still produce drama with greater popular appeal. He mounted at the Abbey an English version of Sophocles's *King Oedipus*. This play's dialogue was in prose, and Yeats strove for clarity and vigor. The prose dialogue he fashioned often veered far from ordinary conversation and simple grammatical construction, but he did produce what remains, seventy years later, the most actable and speakable English adaptation of Sophocles.

David R. Clark and James McGuire's compilation of the play's various manuscripts reveals that Yeats labored as painstakingly over this play's prose as he did over the verse of *At the Hawk's Well,* or *Purgatory.* Examination of the play's drafts and of the versions produced at the Abbey and subsequently published reveals that, within the necessary limits of prose, he achieved through sound, rhythm, metaphor and syntax a dramatic speech nearly as rich in imaginative suggestion as the verse of his dance plays.

An early draft of the priest's speech shows Yeats struggling with the rather stiff, over-literary diction of the Victorian translation from which he was working.

> Oedipus, ruler of my land, you see our ages who are about your door: some but nestlings, tender for far flights, some bowed with age, priests as I of Zeus, and these the chosen youth, while the rest of the people are sitting with wreath branches in the marketplaces, for the city is now too sorely vexed, and can no longer lift up her head from beneath the ways of death.[4]

Yeats was to spend much of his working life clearing out of his writing such literary ornament as "nestlings tender for far flights," and this phrase would be cleared out long before the speech was spoken on a stage or published in a book. The literary "youth," was almost immediately changed to the conversationally serviceable "young men," and "Oedipus, ruler of my land" became "Oedipus, king of my country."

This last change makes for improvements in rhythm and sound. In "ruler of my land" the first and fifth syllables are strongly stressed. In "king of my country" the first and fourth syllables are stressed. Two rather than three unstressed syllables come between the accented syllables, making for greater rhythmic tautness. In Yeats's best writing for the ear, he rarely allows more than two unstressed syllables to fall between his accented syllables. Even when, as in this play, he is writing in prose, he retains his poet's exact time sense. Indeed, the phrase with which the priest's speech begins in its revised form contains three strong stresses. Each of the first two stressed syllables is followed by two quick, unstressed syllables. "*Oed*ipus, *king* of my *coun*try" closely resembles in cadence the three-beat line Yeats developed for the opening songs in *At the Hawk's Well*, and *The Dreaming of the Bones*. Yeats used this same three-beat line, with no more than two unstressed syllables falling between any pair of stressed syllables for "Easter, 1916," one of his most rhythmically compelling poems.

The change from "ruler of my land" to "king of my country" illustrates as well Yeats's use of sound in writing for the voice and the ear. "Ruler of my land" is dominated by liquid sounds, as opposed to the alliterated initial percussives of "king" and "country." Yeats makes extensive use in his dramatic writing of repeated hard unvoiced or semi-voiced consonants, preferring the initial sounds of "beat" "call" or "pallor" to the initial sounds of "ruler" or "horse." In rewriting he tends to substitute plosives for liquids at every opportunity.

The results of Yeats's attention to sound, rhythm, and syntax can be measured when one compares the priest's speech as Yeats drafted it in 1912 with the same speech as it was finally spoken from the Abbey stage:

> Oedipus, king of my country, we who stand before your door are of all ages; some too young to have walked so many miles, some, priests of Zeus such as I, too old. Among us stand the pick of the young men, and behind in the market-places the people throng, carrying suppliant branches. We all stand here because the city stumbles towards death, hardly able to raise up its head. (CPL 304)

In addition to such improvements in sound and rhythm as I have been discussing, one can observe a strengthening of the verbs. In the early draft, people are sitting in the market-place, while in the later, they throng to the market-place and stand before Oedipus. The early draft's city that "is sorely vexed" is in less urgent need than the stage version's city that "stumbles toward death." In the myriad drafts of all his dramatic writing, the verbs strengthen steadily as Yeats moves toward his final version.

The earliest draft of the priest's speech continues as follows:

> A blight has fallen upon the fruitful blossoms of the land, upon the herds, among the pastures; that flaming god descends.[5]

Yeats immediately changed "that flaming god" to "plague." Characteristically, he eschewed a literary figure and used instead the monosyllable with its load of emotional associations. He also changed his verb. "Descends" became "ravages." The new verb, as often in Yeats's dramatic writing, calls for a strong emphasis on its first syllable. The resulting phrase has a similar effect on the ear as that of a spondee in a line of verse: one strong stress follows another. "*Plague ra*vages the city."

The speech in its final form reads as follows:

> A blight has fallen upon the fruitful blossoms of the land; a blight upon flock and field, and upon the bed of marriage. Plague ravages the city. (CPL 304)

The plosive initial sound of "Blight" strikes the ear twice, like a pair of hammer blows. In changing "herds" and "pastures" in the earlier draft to "flock and field," Yeats achieves a second alliteration. "Bed" alliterates with "blight," giving a third hard plosive sound to the sentence. By placing the marriage-bed at the end of the list of blighted things, Yeats gives the impression of an ascending series of disasters, each one more difficult to bear than its predecessor. The priest's speech performs its dramatic function with economy and power. It describes the circumstances that lead to the great moments of passion and invites its hearers to care about those circumstances.

Watching the play take shape through its various drafts, one can observe the advocate of speaking and listening in conflict with the man of letters. Time and again, the worn-out literary phrase is replaced by a resonant, vigorous locution. "In good season" becomes "at the right moment," "those regions" becomes "that very spot," and "draws near" gives place to "comes." In an early draft, Oedipus has the line: "From what man among men was my father?" This evolves into a question that a living speaker might ask: "Who was my father?"

Strong verbs are needed in Oedipus's description of the actions that had led to Laius's death. The early draft of the passage reads:

> The man that came in front and the old man himself would have had me pushed from off the path, and in my anger, I pushed the man that

> pushed me, the driver. The old man, seeing what I had done, waited till I was passing him, and then brought down his two-pronged goad upon my head. I paid him back in full, for I struck him from the carriage with a swift blow of my stick. He rolled on his back, and after that I killed them all.[6]

Yeats immediately changed "pushed" to "struck" and he crossed out "swift." He saw and heard that the passage would derive its strength from verbs rather than adjectives, and he preferred the more decisive "struck" to "pushed." The grammar is simplified and tautened. "In my anger, I pushed the man that pushed me, the driver" becomes "I struck the driver in my anger." The awkward apposition is eliminated, and the necessary verb is moved to the beginning of the phrase. Even the weapon of choice, the "two-pronged goad," is eliminated. The act of violence, expressed in the repeated verb, dominates the speech. Stripped of adjectives and of all but the most necessary nouns, the speech moves from "force" to "struck" to "knock" to "roll" to "kill."

> The man who held the reins and the old man himself would not give me room, but thought to force me from the path, and I struck the driver in my anger. The old man, seeing what I had done, waited till I was passing him, then struck me upon the head. I paid him back in full, for I knocked him out of the carriage with a blow of my stick. He rolled on his back. And after that I killed them all. (CPL 316)

Yeats was constantly battling with the fear that only in a recognized classic like *King Oedipus* could he achieve lasting stage success, because he was always striving to give his characters a vivid speech in the face of the increasing drabness of modern idiom. One can detect in his later writings on the theater an enormous regret that, no matter how gifted the poet and how skilful the performers, verse drama would never again take the ear of a large audience. As he observed in an essay published with *At the Hawk's Well*, his muses would rarely be more than half welcome in an ordinary theater (VPL 415).

At the Hawk's Well first performed 1916

The new aristocratic form of drama he invented with *At the Hawk's Well* and the plays that followed it would appeal, if at all, to audiences who had shut neither their lips nor their ears on poetry. More important, this new form would bring the theater closer to its origins in ritual: "I hope to have attained the distance from life which can make credible strange events, elaborate words" (E and I 221). The new form also freed him to exercise the metrical and rhythmic variations which he knew to be a source of his poetic strength. As he was to note years later:

> There was something in what I felt about Deirdre, about Cuchulain, that rejected the Renaissance and its characteristic metres, and this was the principal reason why I created in dance plays the form that varies blank verse with lyric metres. (E and I 523)

Even in the early drafts of the opening song for *At the Hawk's Well*, he had decided upon the three-beat line, with up to two unstressed syllables preceding and following each accented syllable, from which he was to derive such power in the plays and poems he wrote during these years. Richard Taylor has demonstrated that Yeats, in plays like *At the Hawk's Well* and poems like "Easter, 1916," combined syllabic meter with the more ancient "strong stress" rhythm, and that he achieved an extension or loosening of strict iambic patterns through the addition of extra unstressed syllables. Drawing upon Derek Attridge's work on metrics, Taylor presents a complex system of notation that, like a musical score, graphically sets forth the patterns of stress and release in the lines.[7]

> I sing of the desolate places
> And men that have their fair share;
> The pallor of ivory faces,
> Their lofty, desolate air,
> Have travelled until they die.
> At the day's close, they but find
> A well long choked up and dry
> And boughs long stripped by the wind.[8]

Four of these eight lines had nearly reached the form they would retain in the produced and published version. Nonetheless, the passage seems flaccid and drifting, despite the compelling three-beat lines. One can scarcely hear in this rather conventional choric description the passage that was to convince the young T. S. Eliot that Yeats was indeed a modern poet. The passage is weakened by the flat, rather commonplace lines: "And men that have their fair share," or "Have travelled until they die." One feels that Yeats is using these lines simply to fill in his stanza, to mark place and time, until he finds the means of knitting his song together and giving it force and direction.

As is only appropriate in drama, the song is given direction when Yeats finds the proper framing action, signaled by the proper vigorous verb. Yeats changed the early draft's "sing" with its initial sibilance, to "call" with its initial percussive. "Call" carries its older sense of "conjure" or "evoke." Like the magicians who people so many of Yeats's own juvenilia, the musicians at this play's opening engage in an act of conjuration. By the time the stanza concludes, the spectators are to ignore the evidence of their senses and see what the musicians command them to see. The three-beat lines take on the nature of a spell or incantation.

> I call to the eye of the mind
> A well long choked up and dry
> And boughs long stripped by the wind.
> And I call to the mind's eye
> Pallor of an ivory face,
> Its lofty, dissolute air;
> A man climbing up to a place
> The salt sea wind has swept bare.
>
> (CPL 136)

All Yeats's changes, as the passage moves from early draft toward final version, tend toward concreteness, intensification of verbs, improvements in rhythm. For example the musician in an early draft of the opening song sings of a desolate place. What makes the place desolate? Without a context, desolation is merely another abstraction. The abstraction is made concrete when, in the final version, the listeners hear immediately of the dry well and the stripped boughs. In the early draft, these had been relegated to the stanza's last two lines. The monosyllable "long" occurs in the identical position in the stanza's second and third lines. In both instances, it is the second of three stressed monosyllables.

> A *well long choked* up and dry
> And *boughs long stripped* by the wind.

The repetition and the insistent stresses create the impression of enduring desolation.

Through the drafts of the musician's evocation of the scene's human inhabitants, one can again detect a move toward the concrete. In the first version there are "men," "faces," and "they." In the early draft, the "ivory faces" are introduced as the only concrete detail in a vague picture of otherwise indefinite men. In the final version, the face's pallor creates for the hearer an eerie first impression of a figure about whom nothing else is yet known.

Several other changes, seemingly insignificant in themselves, combine to make substantial contributions to these opening lines. The verb "call" with its percussive initial sound is repeated in the stanza, occupying the first stressed positions in the first and fourth lines. The change from plural to singular, "men" to "man" brings with it a rhythmic improvement. "The pallor of ivory faces" becomes "Pallor of an ivory face." The early version has an unstressed ending: the later version, in changing from plural to singular, gives the line a stressed ending. In the final version, then, each of the eight lines ends with a strongly stressed monosyllable, giving a quality of strength and hardness. Unstressed line endings can create an elegiac, wistful quality, as they do in the play's final song, but they mitigate against the starkness that Yeats is aiming at here. More important, by eliminating the definite article, Yeats moves "pallor" with its strongly stressed initial plosive to the beginning of the line. This becomes the only line in the stanza whose first syllable is accented. In performance, the unexpectedly accented syllable can hit the ear with the force of an explosion. This strong syllable permits Yeats to do something he rarely does in this or any other of his three-beat lines. He inserts three unstressed syllables, the second syllable of "pallor" and the monosyllables "of" and "an" between his two accented syllables. The introduction of more than two unstressed syllables in a row often results in loss of tension. But so strong is the force of the explosion at the beginning of the fifth line that the three quick unstressed syllables create an effect of rhythmic variety, always important to Yeats, with no loss of tautness.

Indeed, in the song's final version, Yeats achieves startling rhythmic variety. Four or perhaps even five of the seven syllables in line 2 take strong stresses. The exact number depends on the performer's interpretation. I would speak the line as follows:

> A *well long choked up* and *dry.*

The line, as well as what it describes, is clogged with heavy hard matter. While a more normal three of the seven syllables in line 4 take strong stresses, two of these, "*mind's eye*," are the last two syllables in the line, and these are followed with no end-stop by the strongly stressed initial plosive of line 5: "*pal*lor."

The lines' syntax combines with their sound and rhythm to create lyric and dramatic power. The initial verb "call" in line 1 is separated by an indirect object from its two direct objects in lines 2 and 3. Each of these objects, "well" and "boughs," is immediately followed by a descriptive phrase, and the respective phrases are identical in both rhythmic and syntactical characteristics: stressed monosyllabic adverb followed by stressed monosyllabic verb. When the verb "call" is repeated in line 4, it is again separated from its direct object, and that object, placed in the startling opening position of line 5, is the quality of a face rather than the face itself. Finally, the indirect object of the verb repeated in lines 1 and 4 varies slightly in form: "the eye of the mind," "the mind's eye." The slight variation suggests the theatrical nature of the musicians' song. The spectators have their actual eyes fixed on a bare space, with perhaps a patterned screen. With their repeated and slightly varying references to the "eye of the mind" the musicians seek, by an act of theatrical evocation, to displace what the audience is actually seeing with an inner vision. In speaking the initial line, I would give additional emphasis to "mind" in order to make clear the distinction from the audience's bodily eyes.

In *At the Hawk's Well*, as in *King Oedipus*, the slow journey from early draft to completed play involves the strengthening of verbs and the consolidation of action. For example, in an early version the rocks, the heart, and the mind all cry for sleep. The various entities longing to sleep give the song a sense of diffusion and attenuation.

> Let me sleep, cry the grey rocks of the steep;
> Let me sleep cries the heart and the mind.
> I am old, and would sleep.[9]

In this draft, several entities are longing for a single action. In the final version a single entity, the heart, is longing for several opposing actions. Diffusion changes to internal conflict.

> The heart would be always awake,
> The heart would turn to its rest.
> . . . .
> Why should I sleep, the heart cries,
> For the wind, the salt wind, the sea wind
> Is beating a cloud through the skies.
> . . . .
> O wind, o salt wind, o sea wind,
> Cries the heart, it is time to sleep.
>
> (CPL 137–38)

These lines figure forth the conflict in the old man's heart. Weary with his long doomed wait, he craves an enduring sleep. At the same time, he knows that he must keep himself in constant wakefulness, or he will miss the well's momentary filling.

The songs bracket descriptions of the Guardian of the Well, and of the old man approaching her. As Bradford and Longenbach have noted, Yeats in these lines of varying lengths approaches free verse. As Richard Taylor demonstrates, "the sliding and indefinite hierarchies of stress have the effect of aural montage and help to suggest the mysterious nature of the well's guardian."[10] Yet even in these passages from which the "ghostly voice" has been all but exorcised, one can detect through the revisions improvements in sound and rhythm, as well as a strengthening of verbs.

"The night is coming on. The mountain side is darkening"[11] gives place to "Night falls. The mountain side grows dark" (CPL 138). The final version features fewer and stronger words, and more active verbs. The Guardian of the Well's weariness is emphasized by repetition, and specificity is imparted to her tasks. In the early draft, she is "too weary with her work clearing the well."[12] In the final form she is "Worn out from raking its dry bed, / Worn out from gathering up the leaves" (CPL 138). Perhaps the most striking improvement comes in the description of what the wind does to the leaves. The early draft reads:

> Nearby, stirred by the falling wind,
> The dry leaves rustle the green,
> And the great heap stirs and flutters.[13]

In the final version, the noun becomes an adjective informed by a verb. The "great heap" becomes "The heaped-up leaves." More

74   PASSIONATE ACTION

important, "stirs and flutters" gives place to an eerie line with a falling rhythm: "They rustle and diminish" (CPL 138).

For the most part, the musicians' language sets forth the inner experience of the persons of the play more powerfully and memorably than does the language of the characters themselves. The blank verse dialogue, always clear and serviceable, rarely achieves the musicians' passionate lyricism. The Cuchulain of this play does not express, and may not yet know, what he has lost. The chorus speaks for him.

> He has lost what may not be found
> Till men heap his burial mound
> And all the history ends.
>
> (CPL 143)

The Dreaming of the Bones completed 1917; performed 1931

In point of blank verse dialogue, *The Dreaming of the Bones* represents an advance over *At the Hawk's Well*. More of the play's verbal power is given to the persons who participate in the action, and less to the musicians who, as the form dictates, must stand outside the action. The play introduces a young revolutionary from the Aran Islands, a survivor of the Easter rising, waiting for rescue. He meets two strangers, a man and a young girl, who offer to take him to the mountaintop he seeks. These strangers slowly reveal that they are the ghosts of King Dermot and Queen Dervorgilla who, seven centuries ago, treacherously opened Ireland to Norman invasion and initiated the long years of oppression. They are doomed to wander through eternity until they find a contemporary Irishman who will forgive them.

The play's early dialogue suggests that the dramatist is less interested in depicting the circumstances from which the passion rises. The young revolutionary speaks neither with the Tudor vocabulary, Gaelic idiom, and astonishing metaphors of Synge, nor with the familiarity of Dublin conversation. In fact, the occasionally strained syntax in the opening passages impedes the living speech of a man.

> I should not be afraid in County Clare.
> *And should be or should not be* have no choice.

> I was in the post-office, *and if taken*,
> I shall be put against a wall and shot.
>
> (CPL 277; italics mine)

These phrases may be an uneasy mix of blank verse with Yeats's attempt at the Aran Islander's idiom. The sort of lyric prose used by Synge might have served this character better.

The masked stranger, dressed in garments of a past time, is better served by blank verse.

> We know the pathways that the sheep tread out
> And all the hiding places of the hills;
> And that they had better hiding places once.
>
> (CPL 278)

The spondee ending the first of these lines suggests a slow pace. By contrast, the young revolutionary's rapidity of speech is suggested by the sharp question and command in his opening lines. "Who is there? I cannot see what you are like. / Come to the light" (CPL 277). When the play is performed, the actors might contrast the stranger's slow, deliberate utterances with the young man's quick, nervous speech. If the voices also contrast in pitch, a high tenor for the young man and a baritone or bass for the stranger, the differences in pitch and pace can be quite effective.

In the ensuing dialogue between the young man and the stranger, Yeats makes repeated use of the divided line. A speech will end with a partial line, which the next speaker will complete at the start of his speech. For all their disparity of appearance and contrast of manner, the high number of shared lines establishes the sense of a strengthening bond between the young man and the stranger. They are members of the same tribe, necessary parts of the same history. More than any other single device, the shared lines suggest that the two figures belong to each other, despite the emerging sense of their growing antagonism. The play's power derives in part from the fusion of antagonism with kinship.

> **STRANGER**   For certain days, the stones where you must lie
> Have in the hour before the break of day
> Been haunted.
> **YOUNG MAN**   But I was not born at midnight.
>
> (CPL 278)

The ten-syllable line, shared by the two speakers, requires a strong stress on "but," which occurs in the stressed fourth position, following the caesura and the unstressed second syllable of "haunted." Because the line's rhythm requires a strong stress on "but," it suggests that the young man is denying the presence of the dead. This sense of denial can be made even stronger if the young man gives an equally strong stress to his next syllable "I." Ever conscious of varying his rhythms, Yeats varies the number of syllables assigned to each speaker in the shared lines. In one case, the young man begins a line with two iambic feet—four syllables. "Come to the light." The phrase is a command. The first foot is inverted, requiring a strong stress on the verb. The stranger completes the line with a question that undermines the tone of command the young man is trying to assume. "But what have you to fear?" (CPL 277) The three perfectly normal iambic feet—unstressed syllable followed by stressed syllable in regular order—contrast with the young man's inversion to create the impression of a calming assurance.

In this case, the young man who begins the line speaks two of its five feet, while the stranger delivers the other three. In the next two cases, the first speaker has three iambic feet. In each case, the partial line that concludes a speech completes a sentence or thought begun in a previous line. Moreover, the penultimate line of each speech is not end-stopped. The responding speaker has a short phrase that completes the line and questions the thought.

> **YOUNG MAN**   I have to put myself into your hands
> Now that my candle's out.
> **STRANGER**   You have fought in Dublin?
>
> (CPL 277)

In another instance, a shared line begins with a question of two iambs and concludes with an answer of three.

> **YOUNG MAN**   What is that sound?
> **STRANGER**   An old horse gone astray.
>
> (CPL 278)

Perhaps the most striking uses of shared lines occur when the young man approaches the subject of betrayal. The stranger interrupts his sentence, completes his line, reiterates a necessary offer of help, and introduces the idea of the returning dead, which is the play's main theme.

> **YOUNG MAN**   But when a man
> Is born in Ireland and of Irish stock,
> When he takes part against us—
> **STRANGER**   I will put you safe.
> No living man shall set his eyes upon you.
> I will not answer for the dead.
>
> (CPL 278)

"Us," the word with which the young man's interrupted speech ends, is the first and unstressed syllable of an iambic foot. "I," with which the stranger's speech begins, as the second syllable of the foot, requires a strong stress. The effective delivery of the passage requires perfect timing from both speakers. In my production of the play, no passage required greater attention to rhythm or more diligent practice.

The two speeches suggest growing conflict. The stranger does not want the young man to think about betrayal. The young man does not yet know that the stranger is the ghost of the arch-traitor who opened the way, seven centuries before the Easter rising, for the Norman conquest of Ireland; he is engaged in an action that seeks to undo the stranger's initial treachery. Each speaker is in absolute opposition to the other. Thus, the performers engage in close cooperation, while the persons the performers represent are in fundamental conflict. Yeats chiefly uses rhythm to communicate this difficult fusion of kinship and conflict. As if to call attention to the difficulty and importance of this passage, the shared line has an extra foot. Set out as a single line of verse, it would read: "When he takes part against us, I will put you safe." This is a six-foot, twelve-syllable line. Creating an extra-long line, an alexandrine, can help a writer of verse emphasize a point. Though hearers rarely count syllables, extra iambic feet can increase the power of the ghostly voice.

A similar change of subject occurs a few speeches later, also marked by a shared line. The young man is talking about the ancient dead, and insisting that they would never betray him. With the words that complete the young man's line, the stranger abruptly changes the subject.

> **YOUNG MAN**   They cannot put me into gaol or shoot me;
> And seeing that their blood has returned to fields
> That have grown red from drinking blood like mine,
> They would not if they could betray.
> **STRANGER**   This pathway
> Runs to the ruined Abbey of Corcomroe;
> The Abbey passed, we are soon among the stone
> And shall be at the ridge before the cocks
> Of Aughanish or Bailevehan
> Or grey Aughtmana shake their wings and cry.
>
> (CPL 279)

The many names lend a Marlovian sonority to this speech that closes the first part of the play. The stranger's murmuring name upon Irish name reinforces an essential kinship between himself and the young man.

Like the ancient Greek tragedies, this play is divided into episodes separated by a chorus. The chorus is a stylized depiction, marked by formal narrative and song, of the climb to the summit of the mountain from which the young man will watch for the coracle that is to take him to the Aran islands. Once aloft, the immediate danger is past, and the lessening of urgency allows for that slowing and stilling which, as Yeats repeatedly argued, are necessary to tragic reverie. Prompted by the lessening of his own danger, by the nearness of the ruined Abbey, and by that sense of the brooding past which place and persons evoke, the young man is ready to put aside his fear and rage, and to ask meditative questions about the anguish of the penitent dead.

> Have those
> Who, if your tale is true, work out a penance
> Upon the mountain top where I am to hide,
> Come from the Abbey grave-yard?
>
> (CPL 280)

From now to the play's end the young girl, who has not previously spoken, will attempt to create in him sufficient distance from immediate events to make forgiveness possible. The introduction of a new voice, which has had no part in the conflict of the previous episode, may make both the young man and the play's hearers more receptive to the new, slower rhythms, the longer sentences, the separation of verb from subject, and the alliteration. Answering the young man's question and completing his line, the young girl speaks of the dead who are doing their penance on the mountain. She distinguishes between the dead of the ruined graveyard, who took part in a more recent rebellion, and the older dead, who committed a more terrible betrayal. In an assonant clause that takes up a single line of blank verse, she gives her first hint at the nature of the crime that exacts so terrible a penance.

> Being but common sinners,
> *No callers-in of the alien from oversea,*
> They and their enemies of Thomond's party
> Mix in a brief dream-battle above their bones;
> Or make one drove; or drift in amity;
> Or in the hurry of the heavenly round
> Forget their earthly names. *These* are a*lone,*
> *Be*ing ac*cursed.*
>
> (CPL 281, my italics)

The assonant line describing the young girl's crime forms an apposition preceding the verb. Here again, the verb's separation by two lines from the subject increases the passage's power. The verb, when it finally comes, occupies the unexpectedly stressed first position of its line. As the young girl's speech continues, a marked pause after "names" and a strong stress on the word that follows it will help the speaker in performance to distinguish the dead of Corcomroe from the more terribly accursed dead. Yeats uses a characteristic rhythmic device to help the speaker make the point. The line consists of three regular iambic feet, with stressed syllable following predictably upon unstressed syllable. After the pause, there is an inverted iamb: "*these* are." The unexpected inversion forces the speaker to lay particular emphasis upon the stressed syllable. Yeats then increases the power by beginning his next line with another inverted iamb. The first syllable of the line takes a strong stress, and that stress is augmented by the syllable's plosive initial sound: "*Be*ing accursed."

The young girl's speech ends with a fragment of a line consisting of two iambs. The young man completes her line, beginning a duet in which, for the most part, each will be completing the other's lines. His speeches heretofore have been characterized by sharp phrases, rapid questions, and sentences that take up a line or less.

Now, in responding to the young girl, he falls into a slower method, uttering a single complex sentence that requires four and a half lines.

> But if what seems is true,
> And there are more upon the other side
> Than on this side of death, many a ghost
> Must meet them face to face, and pass the word
> Even upon this grey and desolate hill.
>
> (CPL 281)

The young man's changing rhythm and sentence structure suggest that he is beginning to partake of her mood. This mood is brought about by lengthening sentences, and by an increasing number of participial phrases and spondees. There is a high incidence of inversion—especially at beginnings of lines, or immediately following caesurae. More often than not, the stressed syllable in the inverted foot has a percussive initial sound. Repeated phrases take on the nature of refrains. Such a phrase, one of several, is the young girl's "being accursed." The phrase describes the lonely ghosts of whom she is speaking, and her speeches are so disposed that it will slowly dawn on the young man and the play's hearers that the two mysterious rescuers, in their heroic masks and their costumes of a past time, are themselves the ghosts of whom she speaks. The phrase gains power in several ways. For one thing, it serves as the concluding, summary phrase of three speeches—each speech revealing more of the ghosts' suffering and penance. Like the refrain to "Easter, 1916" the phrase gains power from sheer repetition. Moreover, although the phrase concludes the speeches in which it occurs, those speeches are so disposed that the phrase is always at the beginning of a line of verse. Thus each speech in which the phrase occurs ends with the fragment of a line which must be completed by the young man. In each case, the Aran revolutionary is drawn more deeply into the ghost's mood and theme, and grows more inclined to share her somber reverie. In performance, the repeated phrase can have a hypnotic insistence.

Each of the young man's speeches in response to the young girl is, like each of her speeches, a single meditative sentence. Subject is separated from verb by a phrase of apposite description. Thus, the details of weariness are inserted between subject and verb when the young girl, speaking of the ghosts whose identity the young man does not yet know, tells him that

> they, weary of life and of men's eyes,
> Flung down their bones in some forgotten place,
> Being accursed.
>
> (CPL 281)

Once again, the grammatical absolute gives additional power to the strong verb, which gains greater strength from its placement as part of a near-spondee at the beginning of a line. In his next speech the young man similarly separates the two halves of a verb phrase when he describes ghosts that "Drive the living, should they meet its face, / Crazy" (CPL 281). Again, the expected word is delayed. When it does occur, it occurs as an inversion with a hard initial sound at the beginning of a line. The listening audience may not be conscious of such niceties of placement, but the hearers will respond to the increased tension and power that a speaker, who must be conscious of such niceties, will give the words. Sharing rhythms and grammatical structures, the young man and the young girl engage in verbal choreography that anticipates the visual choreography in which this play for dancers will climax.

The force accruing to these lines from devices of syntax, sound, and rhythm climaxes in the young girl's simple, one-line reply to the young man's question. "Though eyes can meet, their lips can never meet" (CPL 281). The single line gathers its power from its placement at the end of this shared reverie. In performance it can derive a terrible poignancy from the preceding speeches.

The Aran revolutionary's reply to the ghost's entreaty for forgiveness completes her line and denies her request. Like the young girl's repeated phrase "being accursed," the young man's line and a half is repeated three times from now till the play's end. It too takes on the power of a refrain. Its repeated negatives fall insistently on the ears of the play's hearers, and each negative gains power from the repeated falling rhythms.

> Oh never, never
> Shall Dermot and Dervorgilla be forgiven.
>
> (CPL 283)

Yeats had planned that the climax of the new type of drama he was inventing would take the form of pantomimic dance. True to type, *At the Hawk's Well* had achieved its greatest intensity in the Guardian's dance. In this second of his dance plays, Yeats fashioned a more complex relation between speech and spectacle. The play's climax occurs not in pantomimic dance but rather in the shared reverie in which the young man learns the nature and needs of his strange companions, and elects not to forgive them. His hammering negatives shatter the reverie and bring about the play's turning point.

The dance of the unforgiven traitors that dominates the play's closing moments is not so much climax as dramatic epilogue. Watching the dance, the young man fuses description of their movements with questions expressing his growing apprehension. The speech might be most effective in performance if the young man pauses after each question, expecting an answer that does not come.

> Why do you dance?
> Why do you gaze and with so passionate eyes
> One on the other, and then turn away
> Covering your eyes, and weave it in a dance?
> Who are you? What are you? You are not natural.
> (CPL 283)

The dramatic interest is not predicated exclusively on the dance, as it is at the parallel point in *At the Hawk's Well*. The play in performance forces the audience to attend both to the movements and to their effect on the unforgiving speaker. The young man's repeated utterance "so strangely and so sweetly" (CPL 283) suggests that he is once again almost yielding and tendering the forgiveness these unhappy ghosts implore. The young girl's repeated "seven hundred years" works on his and on the spectators' sympathies.

During the first part of the dance, the speaker's relation is with the dancers. He uses the interrogative mode, gaining power from accumulating questions much as does the speaker of "No Second Troy." During the second part of the dance the young revolutionary, without diminishing the strength and complexity of his relations to the dancers, establishes a dramatic relation to the spectators as well. We have seen that the musicians in *At the Hawk's Well* conjure visions to the spectators' inner eyes, visions which must almost displace, or at least complement, the drawing-room, the patterned screen or cloth, and the masked players at which the spectators are actually gazing. As the doomed couple completes this round of its eternal dance, the young man engages in a similar act of conjuration.

> All the ruin,
> All, all their handiwork is blown away,
> As though the mountain air had blown it away,
> Because their eyes have met.
>
> (CPL 283)

By an act of will, reinforced by the repetitions of "all" and "away," the young man is inducing the spectators to see in vision an Ireland restored, as if the treachery that had brought about the ruin had never been committed. In performance, the speaker's voice can lift and brighten as he utters these triumphant, affirmative lines. Then, with a dramatic modulation, the speaker loses the vision.

> The dance is changing now. They have dropped their eyes.
> They have covered up their eyes, as though their hearts
> Had suddenly been broken. Never never
> Shall Dermot and Dervorgilla be forgiven!
>
> (CPL 284)

In performance the voice can deepen and darken, lowering its pitch as it describes the change in the dance.

After the dancers leave the stage, the young man utters a two-line confession to the audience. The second line begins with an inverted iamb, forcing an added emphasis upon the word. The line also makes use of alliteration, from which power accrues to the word that best describes the young man's experience.

> I had almost yielded, and forgiven it all;
> Terrible the temptation and the place.
>
> (CPL 284)

Purgatory first performed 1938

A key to successful dramatic writing is the creation of a compelling situation and of characters whose passions and conflicts press urgently for expression. By the time he composed *The Dreaming of the Bones*, the playwright was achieving mastery over plot and thought, as well as over diction and song. *Purgatory* demonstrates even greater mastery over all the elements of drama. The play's diction is all the more striking since it arises naturally from plot and thought. In its composition, this tragedy illustrates an Aristotelian prescription.

> In constructing the plot and working it out with the proper diction, the poet should place the scene, as far as possible, before his eyes. In this way, seeing everything with the utmost vividness, as if he were a spectator of the action, he will discover what is in keeping with it.[14]

Bradford describes the excitement communicated by the manuscripts. "The impetus of the vision Yeats saw is cast on to the reader by the half-formed words that seem at times literally to have been hurled on to the page."[15]

For this play Yeats abandoned blank verse, using instead a four-beat line with a varying number of unaccented syllables preceding and following each stressed syllable. An occasional five-beat line in the midst of a speech forces the speaker to slow down, or to emphasize a thought or image. Like blank verse, the four-beat lines give the play's words both heightening and deep stability.

In the final moments of *Purgatory*, the old man's contemplation of his mother's new-won purity is interrupted by the hoofbeats that bring with them the certainty that her soul has not been released.

> I killed that lad because had he grown up
> He would have struck a woman's fancy,
> Begot, and passed pollution on.
> I am a wretched foul old man,
> And therefore harmless. When I have stuck
> This old jackknife into a sod
> And pulled it out all bright again,
> And picked up all the money that he dropped,
> I'll to a distant place and there
> Tell my old jokes among new men.
> Hoofbeats! Dear God
> How quickly it returns—Beat—beat!
>
> (CPL 435)

Powerful effects derive from the repetition of "hoofbeats" and "beat." The repeated semi-voiced plosives strengthen the audience's sense of the mother's suffering and her son's rage. In an early draft, Yeats had written "horsehoofs."[16] The apparently small change to "hoofbeats" suggests that he continued to favor repeated, percussive consonants.

An earlier draft of the old man's account of his reasons for killing his son reads:

> I killed that lad because of his youth.
> He would soon take some woman's fancy,
> Beget and pass pollution on.[17]

Rewriting the passage, Yeats changed his verb tenses and strengthened his verbs. "Take" became "struck" a word stronger in sound as well as sense. The change from "beget" to "begot" forces the speaker's mouth to open slightly wider in pronouncing the word, thereby creating a fuller sound. The change is tiny, but it represents the difference between adequacy and distinction. The repeated percussives "bright," "begot," "passed pollution," and the penultimate line's "appease" lend their plosive force to the sense of terrible life pressing for expression through the insistent, four-beat lines. In its luminous dance of strong syllables, the speech glorifies the voice that utters it and rewards the ears that hear it.

3
Reshaping the Plot

All through your wanderings, the doors of kings
Shall be thrown wider open, the poor men's hearths
Heaped with new turf, because you are wearing this
To show that you have Deirdre's story right.

—*Deirdre*

Shortly after the Irish National Theatre had established itself at the Abbey, Yeats sent a pamphlet called "Advice to Playwrights" to anyone who might want to write for the new company. He advised prospective dramatists that a play

> must possess a unity unlike the accidental profusion of nature.... the attainment of this unity by what is usually a long shaping and reshaping of the plot is the principal labour of the dramatist, and not the writing of the dialogue.[1]

As with many of the dramatist's prescriptions, he was offering this advice as much to himself as to the novice playwrights to whom it was putatively addressed. During repeated revisions of *The Shadowy Waters*, *On Baile's Strand*, and *Deirdre* undertaken between 1905 and 1908, the apprentice playwright consciously set out to "arrange much complicated life into a single action" (EXP 108). His success with dramatic language and the depiction of passionate personality would depend entirely on his mastery of plot, for him the drama's most intractable element. He wrote Arthur Symons that "one thing I am now quite sure of is that all the finest poetry comes logically out of the fundamental action" (L 460). Laboring far from ecstasy during the contentious second half of his most active Abbey decade, Yeats taught himself the truth of Aristotle's famous pronouncement on *mythos*. "The most powerful elements of emotional interest in Tragedy—*Peripeteia* or reversal of the situation, and Recognition scenes—are parts of the plot."[2]

Like Sophocles, Shakespeare, and Racine, Yeats found that he would rather reshape existing stories, already rich in mythical associations, than add to his difficulty by inventing new stories. From the time he began work on *The Wanderings of Oisin*, he had been attracted to ancient Irish legends. Augusta Gregory's retelling of these legends provided him with a treasure house of material that he would be drawing on to the end of his life.

Gregory's *Cuchulain of Muirthemne*, bringing together most of the stories of the Red Branch cycle, was first published in 1902. Yeats hailed the book as the "best that has come out of Ireland in my time" (CM 11). It was to stand in the same relation to his plays that Hollinshed's Chronicles or North's Plutarch stood in relation to Shakespeare's. From the time of the book's publication to the time of Yeats's last play, published posthumously and first performed eleven years after the playwright's death, Yeats the dramatist would turn to Gregory's book for stories.

On Baile's Strand first performed 1904; revised 1906

The first of these stories on which Yeats founded a play was "The Only Son of Aoife," a tale in which Cuchulain unknowingly kills his only son. Yeats's dramatization of this story would become *On Baile's Strand* whose first performance, sharing a bill with Gregory's farce *Spreading the News*, would open the new Abbey Theatre in December, 1904.

Gregory's retelling begins with a recapitulation of Cuchulain's fight in Scotland with the warrior-queen Aoife. "He left Aoife, the queen he had overcome in battle, with child; and when he was leaving her, he told her what name to give the child" (CM 237). But Cuchulain, returning to Ulster, courts and marries Emer. When Aoife learns of his betrayal, she resolves to bring up their son with the sole purpose of killing his father. When the son reaches manhood, she sends him to Ireland, first laying three commands, or *geasas*, upon him. These are never to give over in a fight, but to battle any opponent to the death; never to refuse combat, no matter whom the challenger; and never to give his name or any account of himself, no matter what the provocation.

A *geasa* is an unbreakable bond, mounting almost to an enchantment, that compels any one upon whom it is laid to perform a particular action without fail. As Yeats was to discover in fashioning these ancient legends for the stage, the *geasa* could be a useful plot device in epic, but it could become problematic in drama. Though *geasas* were prominent in all the Cuchulain stories that Yeats made into plays, he rarely allowed them to serve as motives for his dramatis personae. He was greatly to alter the reasons for the young man's actions.

Arriving at Ulster while the High King Conchubar is in council, the young man kills Conall, one of Conchubar's best warriors and Cuchulain's good friend. Thirsty for revenge, Cuchulain fights the young man.

> The flames of the hero light began to shine about his head; and by that sign, Conlaoch knew him to be Cuchulain his father; and just at that time he was aiming his spear at him. And when he knew it was Cuchulain, he threw his spear crooked, that it might pass beside him; but Cuchulain threw his spear . . . and it struck the lad in the side and went into his body that he fell to the ground . . . Conlaoch showed the ring that was on his hand and he said "Come here while I am lying on the field. . . . I am Conlaoch son of the hound. (CM 239)

Conchubar observes Cuchulain's terrible grief and rage.

> "There is trouble on Cuchulain," said Conchubar. "He is after killing his own son. And if I and all my men were to go against him, by the end of the day he would destroy every man of us. Go now," he said to Scathbad the druid, "and bind him to go down to Baile's Strand and to give three days' fighting against the waves of the sea, rather than to kill us all."
>
> . . . And he fought with the waves three days and three nights, till he fell from hunger and weakness.
>
> (CM 241)

Rich in dramatic irony and climaxing in tragic recognition, the story of Cuchulain's fight with his son cries out for the stage. In preparing it for the new Abbey's stage, Yeats immediately began to alter it. After the episodic *Countess Cathleen*, he had got into the habit of confining each of his plays to a single location and a single action. Confining the action to the climactic confrontation at Baile's Strand, the playwright had to invent means to tell the audience about Aoife's hatred of Cuchulain and the early history of the fighting man's son. More difficult alterations were necessary in making the conflict between father and son stageworthy. Frank Fay, who would be playing Cuchulain, was skilled in stage combat, but Yeats, always distrustful of unchoreographed movement on stage, probably did not want the climax of the first poetic play performed in the new theater to be a wordless swordfight. This was to be a perennial problem in every Cuchulain play. In all the stories, Cuchulain's speech is in his sword. Yeats always needed to make occasion for Cuchulain and his adversaries to talk passionately and lyrically. Yeats also preferred to follow the Greek and the French dramatists by moving his most violent action offstage. Thus, he had to fashion a climactic scene involving father and son that would lead to an offstage fight.

To do this, he devised two dramatic strategies. First, he expanded on the hint, given in Gregory's prose narrative, of an inchoate bond between father and son. In her narrative, the young man tells Cuchulain that, were he not under command not to give his name to anyone, there is "no man in the world I would sooner give it to than yourself since I saw your face" (CM 239). In Yeats's dramatization, it is Cuchulain, and not the young man, who initiates the offer of friendship. Yeats's Cuchulain, unlike Gregory's, has no idea that he has fathered a son upon Aoife. He grieves in the belief that he is childless. Yet seeing the resemblance between the stranger and Aoife, the woman he had once loved, he feels mysteriously drawn to the young man. The scene's poignancy is increased when Yeats, departing from Gregory, has his hero offer the young man a cloak that he had received from his own father.

> My father gave me this.
> He came to try me, rising up at dawn
> Out of the cold dark of the rich sea.
> He challenged me to battle, but before
> My sword had touched his sword, told me his name,
> Gave me this cloak, and vanished.
>
> (CPL 175)

Knowing Cuchulain's true relation to the young man, a theater audience will be moved to pity and dread by the terrible ironies inherent in these lines.

Having created so strong and eerie a bond between Cuchulain and his unknown son, the playwright must invent the situation that credibly brings about their offstage fight. Consequently, he expands the role of Conchubar and creates dramatic conflict between the high king and his greatest warrior. This conflict between characteristically Yeatsian opposites drives the play. In Gregory's narrative, Cuchulain himself insists on fighting the young stranger. In the play, it is Conchubar who opposes Cuchulain's burgeoning alliance with this unknown emissary of Aoife, whom he deems an enemy. Asserting his right to this friendship, Cuchulain commits an unthinkably treasonous act: he attacks the high king. Convinced that he has been bewitched and that the young stranger is allied with supernatural enemies, he drives his former protege and new adversary to an offstage fight.

Cuchulain's recognition that the man he has killed is his own son and his deluded battle with the waves are givens of the story. The dramatist does not alter them, but he determines how they are best to be revealed on the stage. In the narrative, the *anagnorisis* occurs when the dying young man shows Cuchulain his armring—the same armring that Cuchulain had given to Aoife. Yeats, at first, simply recast this event in dialogue. Maud Gonne, ever loyal to the ancient epics, preferred this to his subsequent alterations.

> The Cuchulain play is very much improved since I heard it, but I can't help regretting one of the previous endings, when the body of the young man was brought in, and Cuchulain recognised him as he lay dying. This ending is more original but less strong, I think.[3]

In departing from the epic, Yeats was moving toward a dramatic exploration of folly and blindness. As Cuchulain and the young man fight offstage, one of three singing women who serve as a chorus observes: "Life drifts between a fool and a blind man to the end / And nobody can know his end" (CPL 178). Acting as coauthors, as they had in *Cathleen ni Houlihan,* Yeats and Gregory gave theatrical concreteness to this idea by inventing a fool and a blind man whose relations and tensions shadow those of Cuchulain and Conchubar. This invention may have had a practical motive. The Abbey directors would want to write into the play a prominent part for Willy Fay, who had demonstrated his comic genius and who, for the "beautiful fantasy of his playing in the part of the fool" was to be the dedicatee of the published play. But theatrical practicality merged with what Yeats must have perceived as a deep metaphoric need. In a theatrical tour de force, it is the fool and the blind man who reveal to Cuchulain, in oblique and piecemeal fashion, the identity of the young man he has just killed. This revelation gains in power because the dramatist, continuing to depart from his narrative source, keeps Cuchulain ignorant of the existence of Aoife's son until this moment.

> **BLIND MAN**   He was a queen's son.
> **CUCHULAIN**   What queen? What queen? . . .
> **FOOL** He said a while ago that the young man was Aoife's son.
> **CUCHULAIN**   She?
> No! no! She had no son when I was there.
> **FOOL**   That blind man there said that she owned him for her son.
> **CUCHULAIN**   I had rather he had been
> Some other woman's son. What father had he?
>
> (CPL 180)

Yeats fashions a scene of quiet, mounting terror that climaxes in tragic recognition and requires no theatrical pyrotechnics. It unfolds entirely in dialogue—the fool and blind man's prose counterpointing Cuchulain's verse.

In Gregory's retelling of the fight with the sea, as in Yeats's poem more than a decade earlier, Cuchulain had been enchanted by a Druid at Conchubar's command. But Yeats now reshaped the events of the scene to reveal a loveless man, desperately needing the affection of the young stranger, who responded with sudden violence to perceived betrayal. Such a figure would need no enchantment to engage the waves in battle; indeed enchantment, by divorcing Cuchulain from responsibility for his actions, would diminish the tragic effect. The blind man's insight coupled with his need for the fool's description motivates and cues the choric scene.

> **FOOL**   O, he is fighting the waves.
> **BLIND MAN**   He sees King Conchubar's crown in every one of them.
>
> (CPL 181)

From the young stranger's first entrance to the final offstage battle with the waves, Yeats had shaped a dramatic action of considerable power. But he himself was unsatisfied with the play that opened at the newly established Abbey Theatre on December 27, 1904. In that version, the young stranger enters about halfway through the play.

Preceding his entrance, much of the action is taken up with the assembly of kings at Baile's Strand. The 1904 play gives the assembled kings no strong reason for being there, and never credibly connects their activity to the encounter between Cuchulain and his unknown son. For most of the scene, Cuchulain banters with the younger men, while Conchubar conducts business with the older ones. There are a few poignant moments as Cuchulain wistfully discusses fathers and children (VPL 488), but these are all but lost amid talk of plans to rebuild the burned city, of Usnach's children, of shipments of bronze and wood coming from over the sea, or of the wonders of Aoife's country. The scene is marred by split focus, old men on one side, young men on the other, with Cuchulain and Conchubar occasionally throwing barbs at each other across the stage. Much of the first half of *On Baile's Strand,* in the version performed at the Abbey in 1904, seems to be marking time until the young stranger's entrance.

Yeats worked at the play for the next eighteen months, producing a substantially revised and greatly improved version at the Abbey in April, 1906. In this version, Yeats added to his depiction of Cuchulain's growing conflict with his son a new extended scene in which High King Conchubar attempts to bind Cuchulain to an oath of fealty. Conchubar's desire to domesticate his greatest warrior gave the Assembly of Kings in the play's revised version a new purpose whose dramatic working out would reveal with Sophoclean irony Cuchulain's tragic ambivalence about his lack of a son. "Conchubar is coming today to put an oath upon him that will stop his rambling and make him as biddable as a house-dog" (CPL 163). The consequences of domestication come to dominate the scene. Cuchulain scorns Conchubar's children, and his scorn leads to a revelation of his inner conflict about his apparent childlessness.

> **CUCHULAIN** Conchubar, I do not like your children;
> They have no pith, no marrow in their bones,
> And will lie soft where you and I lie hard.
> **CONCHUBAR** You rail at them
> Because you have no children of your own.
> **CUCHULAIN** I think myself most lucky that I leave
> No pallid ghost or mockery of a man
> To drift and mutter in the corridors
> Where I have laughed and sung.
>
> (CPL 167–68)

Audiences of the reshaped play are made to perceive a Cuchulain who shuns the diminishment that he believes comes with age and fatherhood, yet who obsessively desires a son who will prove worthy of him. This sense of Cuchulain, inchoate and confused in the play's 1904 version, is brought into precise dramatic focus by the reshaped events of the version first performed in 1906.

The driving ideas of domestication and childlessness are amplified and reinforced in the revised expository scene between the fool and the blind man. Coauthored by Yeats and Gregory, this scene of grotesque prose comedy is intricately woven into the fabric of the verse tragedy. In a stunning metadramatization, the blind man seats himself in Conchubar's chair and, taking for the moment the role of Conchubar, addresses the Fool who is, for the moment, aping Cuchulain's incipient biddability.

> What sons have you to pay your debts, and to put a stone over you when you die? Take the oath, I tell you; take a strong oath! (CPL 163)

Yeats's revisions of *On Baile's Strand* may constitute his greatest single advance in plot construction. But such dramatic winnowing as he engaged in during the hard months of work on this play never came easily to the dramatist. He wrote his father: "A play looks easy but is full of problems which are almost a part of mathematics" (L 649). Yeats would have agreed with Lukacs, who had written that "the drama comes to be built upon mathematics—a complicated web of abstraction."[4]

The always present necessity of logic offended what Yeats most dearly valued in poetry. Throughout his writings, he extolled the crooked road of intuition as opposed to the straight road of logic. He excoriated the "hawk of the mind" flying straight to its object, and declared that "wisdom is a butterfly, not a gloomy bird of prey" (CP 159). One of the things he most valued in Gregory's retellings of the Cuchulain legends was the profusion of miraculous incident that he had to excise when he came to dramatize them. In his preface to her book, he used Aristotle's famous terms of probability and necessity, the foundations of that logical plot construction he admired and hated, to signal his chafing against Aristotle. "We find as we expect in the work of men who were not troubled by any probabilities or necessities but those of emotion itself an immense variety of incident and character and of ways of expressing emotion" (CM 15).

The revised *On Baile's Strand* places the passion and precision of verse in the service of a fundamental dramatic action. But this action unfolds through three related stories. Despite Yeats's skill in fusing these stories, he knew he had written a play vulnerable to the accusation of over-complexity. Indeed, he had his fool wittily anticipate such a response from the audience. "You were telling me one story, and now you are telling me another story; how can I get the hang of it at the end if you mix everything at the beginning?" (CPL 165). Some contemporary productions, such as an April 1999 staging by Trinity Repertory, excise the whole business of Conchubar's binding Cuchulain to an oath, and proceed directly from the fool and blind man's opening repartee to the young stranger's entrance. This solution may work best, as in Trinity's case, when the play is done as part of the entire Cuchulain cycle—that is, when some or all of the Cuchulain plays, composed at different times and for different theatrical resources, are performed as a single evening of theater. For all its power, the reshaped play remains problematic. The playwright ruefully recognized this in a preface published with the 1906 version, written before he had composed any other Cuchulain plays. "It is now as right as I can make it with my present experience, but it must always be a little over-complicated when played by itself" (VPL 526).

Deirdre first performed 1906; revised 1908

Deirdre is the playwright's attempt at greater simplicity of action. For this play Yeats drew again on Gregory's prose narratives. "Fate of the Sons of Usnach," one of the best known and most innately dramatic ancient legends of the Red Branch warriors, is a sprawling narrative of elopement, exile, and betrayal. Adhering to the Sophoclean model, Yeats composed a single continuous action, depicting only the lovers' return from Scottish exile and their catastrophe. The ancient tragic rhythm, as many critics point out, moves from purpose through passion to perception.[5] *Deirdre* is the first of many plays in which Yeats focuses on the final stage, the visionary and tragic moment of perception—of Aristotelian recognition.

The playwright made a number of alterations, inventions, and deletions, but one incident he could not alter was Gregory's depiction of the encounter between Deirdre, her lover Naoise, and the

3 / RESHAPING THE PLOT

king's messenger Fergus. In both the narrative and the resulting play, Fergus is Conchubar's predecessor as high king, and a man who has earned the trust of all the great heroes of Ulster. It falls to this character, whom Yeats describes in the notes to the play as "a mixture of chivalry and folly" (VPL 389), to lure the lovers home from Scotland. In response to Fergus's tempting embassy, Deirdre memorably foresees all that is to follow.

> "I see Conchubar asking for blood; I see Fergus caught with hidden lies; I see Deirdre crying with tears, I see Deirdre crying with tears." (CM 102)

What is best in Yeats's play, the heroine's passionate lyricism, is embryonically present in these lines from Gregory's narrative. The play's major flaw is embryonically present as well in Gregory's rendering of Fergus's reply.

> "A thing that is unpleasing to me and that I would never give into," said Fergus, "is to listen to the howling of dogs and to the dreams of women. And since Conchubar the high king has sent a message of friendship it would not be right for you to refuse it." (CM 102)

This exchange between Deirdre and Fergus makes for Yeats's most insuperable problem of dramatization. For the story's sake it is necessary for Naoise to ignore Deirdre's fears and, in the face of all common sense and at the disregard of a seven-year marriage, act on the mere strength of a promise offered by a man he has no reason to trust. Unable to alter this material in a story well known to his audience, Yeats could not prevent the intrusion into his play of something not quite human.[6] He worked and reworked the tense scenes in which Naoise bats away at Deirdre's reasonable fears, but these scenes, for all his attention, remain the play's least successful passages.

> **DEIRDRE** There's none to welcome us.
> **NAOISE** Being his guest,
> Words that would wrong him can but wrong ourselves.
> **DEIRDRE** An empty house upon the journey's end.
> Is that the way a king that means no mischief
> Honours a guest?
> . . . .

> **NAOISE** . . .
> We must not speak or think as women do,
> That when the house is all abed, sit up
> Marking among the ashes with a stick
> Till they are terrified. Being what we are,
> We must meet all things with an equal mind.
>
> (CPL 118)

This passage typifies the structural flaw in the action. The story made it necessary for Naoise to belittle and reject Deirdre's warnings and apprehensions, and nothing the playwright could do in reworking Naoise's scenes could make him a dramatically credible antagonist for the personage Yeats termed "the Irish Helen" (VPL 389).

Yeats chafes against the imposed limits both of the story and of the deliberately concentrated dramatic form he has chosen.

> In arranging the story for the bounds of a one-act play, I have had to leave out many details, even some important persons, that are in all the old versions. . . . The principal difficulty with the form of dramatic structure I have adopted is that, unlike the loose Elizabethan form, it continually forces one by its rigour of logic away from one's capacities, experiences and desires, until, if one have not patience to wait for the mood, or to rewrite again and again till it comes, there is rhetoric and logic and dry circumstance where there should be life. (VPL 389–91)

Yeats's Naoise takes life only after he is convinced of Conchubar's treachery. It remained for Synge, Yeats's superior in psychological invention, to devise a credible motive for the Naisi of his play.[7]

For Yeats the play's fundamental action is the triumph of Deirdre's courage and moral radiance over outer and inner darkness. Accordingly, his most significant alterations concern Deirdre's words and actions, and the setting where these occur. Gregory's narrative places the lovers in the house of the Red Branch while epic battles rage outside. Much of Gregory's story is given over to descriptions of the fighting. As Conchubar's armies weaken, the High King persuades his druid to enchant the sons of Usnach. The Druid raises the semblance of an ocean in which Naisi and his brothers believe themselves to be drowning. They let their swords fall, are captured, and all three are beheaded by a single sword blow.

> Deirdre loosed out her hair and threw herself on the body of Naose before it was put in the grave, and gave three kisses to him, and when her mouth touched his blood, the colour of burning sods came into her cheeks, and she rose up like one that had lost her wits, and she went on through the night till she came to where the waves were breaking on the strand. (CM 114)

After many waverings and vicissitudes, the crazed Deirdre at last obtains a knife.

> She drove the black knife into her side, and she drew it out again, and threw it into the sea to her right hand the way no one would be blamed for her death. (CM 114)

By excising the heroic battles and the Druidic enchantments, Yeats created a quiet lyric tragedy whose single action concentrates on Deirdre's inner journey. For the physical setting of this journey, the playwright invented an isolated guesthouse surrounded by failing light, a setting that serves as a perfect theatrical metaphor.[8] Yeats's Deirdre, unlike Gregory's, does not go wandering; once she enters this house, she never leaves it, and she achieves her tragic apotheosis amid its gathering darkness.

Inhabiting this guesthouse as the play opens are three musicians, also of the playwright's invention. They enable him to give to his play a formal, well cadenced and straightforward exposition, delivered by a powerful voice. The musicians comprise Yeats's first experiment in drama with the sort of lyric chorus that was to become a mainstay of his plays.

Though the enchantments of Gregory's narrative are excised from the stage action, the dramatist embeds in the play's language the sense that there is magic in Conchubar's web. Alone for a few moments on stage with Deirdre, the musicians tell her:

> There are strange miracle-working wicked stones
> Men tear out of the heart and the hot brain
> Of Libyan dragons.
>
> (CPL 120)

Making use of the half-seen armed men and the enchantments described by the musicians, Yeats arranges his action in such a way as to instill in the audience an eerie and terrifying impression of the unseen Conchubar's dark purpose. Deirdre's agony in opposing this purpose is increased because Naoise, who should be her lover and protector, becomes a surrogate for her antagonist.

In the play as Yeats fashions it, the two principal antagonists are Deirdre and Conchubar. Each is attempting to manipulate the other, and the result is a tragedy of mutual gamesmanship. Yeats takes over the game of chess from Gregory's narrative, using it as an effective stage metaphor for the quiet agon he is crafting. One of the playwright's most interesting revisions increases the audience's sense of Conchubar's power and increases as well the emblematic power of the chess game. Naoise must be made to recognize, at a point when he is powerless to act upon the recognition, that Conchubar has in fact betrayed him and that Deirdre's apprehensions have been justified all along. In the play's first version, produced in 1906, the combination of Deirdre's frenzy and the musicians' silent presence cause Naoise to change his mind.

>   **DEIRDRE**   I'll spoil this beauty that brought misery,
>   And houseless wandering on the man I loved.
>   These wanderers will show me how to do it;
>   To clip this hair to baldness, blacken my skin
>   With walnut juice, and tear my face with briars.
>   . . . .
>   Whatever were to happen to my face
>   I'd be myself, and there's not any way
>   But this to bring all trouble to an end.
>   **NAOISE**   What have you told to put such frenzy in her?
>   **FERGUS**   Yes, speak it out.
>   **NAOISE**   I give you my protection,
>   Are you afraid to speak? Does the king love her?
>   Will no one answer?
>   **DEIRDRE**   Tell out all the plot,
>   The spells, the network, all the treachery;
>   Tell of the bridal chamber and the bed,
>   The magical stones, the wizard's handiwork.
>   **NAOISE**   Ah! now I understand why it is you fear
>   To waken death with words. Take care of Deirdre:
>   She must not fall alive into his hands.
>
>   (VPL 395–96)

In the alteration made after Mrs. Patrick Campbell agreed to play Deirdre in 1908, Naoise does not appeal to the musicians. He continues simply to oppose Deirdre until Conchubar, like an unseen chess master, makes his entrapping move.

> **DEIRDRE**   Whatever were to happen to my face,
> I'd be myself, and there's not any way
> But this to bring all trouble to an end.
> **NAOISE**   Leave the gods' handiwork unblotched, and wait
> For their decision. Our decision is past.
> (A dark-faced messenger comes to the threshold)
> **FERGUS**   Peace, peace! The messenger is at the door.
> He stands upon the threshold, he stands there.
> He stands, King Conchubar's purpose on his lips.
> **MESSENGER**   Supper is on the table. Conchubar is waiting for his guests.
> **FERGUS**   All's well again! All's well, all's well!
> You cried your doubts so loud, that I
> Had almost doubted.
> **NAOISE**   We doubted him,
> And he the while but busy in his house
> For the more welcome.
> **DEIRDRE**   The message is not finished.
> ....
> **MESSENGER**   Deirdre and Fergus, son of Rogh, are summoned.
> But not the traitor that bore off the queen.
> It is enough that the king pardon her,
> And call her to his table and his bed.
> **NAOISE**   So then it's treachery.
>
> (CPL 123)

The introduction of Conchubar's agent, this quiet, implacable messenger who contrasts absolutely with the raging Deirdre, makes for a first-rate piece of dramatic invention. It establishes Deirdre and Conchubar as the play's antagonists who manipulate the other figures and each other as if they were all pieces on the chessboard that Yeats makes into one of the play's chief props.

The dramatist's most striking alterations to Gregory's narrative render the chess game an emblem of considerable complexity and power. One such is the skillful weaving of an older story into the dramatic depiction of Deirdre's story. When Naoise and Deirdre enter the guesthouse, Naoise immediately spots a chessboard that is laid out upon a table. This is the board

> Where Lugaidh Redstripe and that wife of his
> Who had a seamew's body half the year
> Played at the chess upon the night they died.
>
> (CPL 117)

In weaving Lugaidh's story into the play, Yeats makes a mirror for Deirdre's story and, in so doing, gives his play the "emotion of multitude" (E and I 215). The very presence of the board is ominous, charging the onstage atmosphere, even in the play's opening moments, with a ritualistic sense of betrayal and noble death. Later, when Naoise and Deirdre realize that there is no hope of escape for them, they adopt Lugaidh and his wife as forbears and deliberately emulate their stoic chess game. Lugaidh Redstripe and his wife are featured in Gregory's prose narratives, but they do not appear in her account of Deirdre. At the beginning of "The Only Jealousy of Emer" a story upon which Yeats would draw for a future play, they are glimpsed playing chess. Yeats turned Lugaidh and his wife—contemporaries of Deirdre and Naoise in Gregory's narrative—into ancient precursors upon whose story Deirdre and Naoise can draw as upon a half-forgotten myth.

In this play of conflict without battle, Yeats invents dramatic devices to render Deirdre a fit opponent for her unseen, seemingly omnipotent antagonist. Part of her dramatic power accrues from the great beauty and commanding presence that are hers in all the ancient legends, and that require for their portrayal a performer of considerable ability. The dramatist increases this power by making of his Deirdre, in contrast to the Deirdre of the narrative, a deliberate player of roles. Throughout the play, Deirdre adopts self-consciously dramatic strategies by which she hopes first to persuade Naoise, and at last to defeat Conchubar. Her strategies, quite as much as Conchubar's schemes, drive the action.

> But the wind's blown upon my hair, and I
> Must set the jewels on my neck and head
> For one that's coming.
> . . . .
> These women have the raddle that they use

> To make them brave and confident, although
> Dread toil or cold may chill the blood of the cheeks.
>   (CPL 116–17)

As Naoise and Fergus talk, the audience sees Deirdre, with the musicians' help, striving to alter herself with jewels and color for Conchubar's arrival. This act of physical transformation becomes as charged an emblem of the ongoing action as does the game of chess.

Eliminating Gregory's battles and epic enchantments, Yeats fashions an action that systematically limits Deirdre's choices, isolates her in nobility from the active men who seem to swirl round her, and drives her to her one possible choice: the final marriage to Naoise in death. The double catastrophe is a given of the narrative, but the playwright invents dramatic details that best suit his purpose. With Naoise ignominiously caught in a net and slaughtered, with Conchubar's half-seen army surrounding the guesthouse, Deirdre's only remaining choice is to persuade the triumphant king to give her the time she will need to end her life in her chosen way. The narrative's epic action is confined in the drama to a few quiet moments in a little room. As the playwright indicated in his praise of Mrs. Patrick Campbell's performance, Deirdre, at the last, experiences and communicates a solitary passion.

It is widely held that the plays for dancers constitute Yeats's breakthrough into maturity as a playwright. Bradford describes the period until 1910 as a long apprenticeship.[9] But the mature playwright could not have achieved what he did in the dance plays had not the apprentice, in the Red Branch plays he was working on between 1904 and 1910, mastered the craft of dramatic plotting. For all the theatrical experimentation of Yeats's maturity, he never abandoned the necessities and probabilities of plot. To the end of his life, he began work on a new play with a scenario, an ordered sense of what was to happen, but he never learned to enjoy plotting. Despite Aristotle's warning that the "poet or 'maker' should be the maker of plots rather than of verses,"[10] Yeats often complained about the dreadful labour of fashioning the scenario (L 511). Even so, he did not choose to experiment with monodrama—as Beckett occasionally did. Neither did he adopt the solution of his friend Ezra Pound.

> I catch the character I happen to be interested in at the moment he interests me, usually a moment of song, self-analysis, or sudden

understanding or revelation. And the rest of the play would bore me and presumably the reader.[11]

Pound did not write plays—choosing instead, like Browning, the dramatic monologue not intended for performance.

Yeats, like Pound, was often bored by the "rest of the play." His discovery with Pound of the Noh led him to a dramatically credible method of leaping to the moment in the play that most engaged his attention, and of using lyric means to convey the necessary background to the audience. Yeats used the Noh very much to his own purposes. Anyone watching a dramatic exhibition by trained Japanese performers will learn more about the Noh than Yeats and Pound ever knew. The Irishman's exuberant ignorance of the Noh freed him to incorporate a few of its devices into his own dramaturgy.[12]

At the Hawk's Well first performed 1916

For his first new play in six years, composed in a revolutionary new form, he turned to a familiar subject, the Red Branch legends as set forth by Augusta Gregory. Though he drew on the personality of Cuchulain as Gregory described it, and as it had been taking shape in his own previous plays, he invented a story instead of appropriating one. He would not in this radical new play be constrained, as in *Deirdre*, to dramatize the events of a known legend. Richard Taylor has argued that the Noh play *The Waters of Immortality* may be a source, at least an analog, for Yeats's play.[13] Yeats may indeed have derived his central situation from this and other Noh plays, but the essential details of the play, the relations among Cuchulain, the Old Man, and the Guardian of the Well, are Yeats's dramatic invention.

Such circumstances and details that might, in more conventional plays, rise out of the central action are stripped away. Yeats's exaltation about this new form he is inventing arises in large part because he perceives himself at last free from the weary world of theatrical apparatus with its complex, encumbering plots. Though Yeats's dramaturgy in this play is notably different from that of his earlier Abbey plays, he adheres to the principle that all must flow from the fundamental action. Every element of this play—the musicians' songs, all the dialogue, the arrangement of the events—contributes to the central idea: the conflict between the growth and decay of life and the stasis of immortality. Similar conflicts inform the Byzantium poems.

This driving idea is revealed through an austere fundamental action. An old man and a young man wait for water that has the power to confer eternal life to bubble briefly in a dry well. The Well's Guardian deceives them, sending one to sleep and alluring the other away from the well. The water plashes, and both men miss it. The old man recognizes that his life has been stolen, and the young man sets out to lead the turbulent life of a flawed hero.

For *At The Hawk's Well* as for *Deirdre*, the dramatist used musicians who could credibly employ a lyric diction and lyric meters. But these musicians do not, as do their counterparts in the first moments of the earlier play, tell the audience a story. Instead, they set the play's dominant tone and direct the order and manner in which the action will unfold. Their ordering of events imparts to this simple story a complex irony. The musicians initially conjure the well "long choked up and dry." They then proceed to reveal to the audience, by their act of folding the cloth, the Guardian and the old man. These figures make visible and audible the blight, weariness, and inchoate malevolence of the musicians' lyrics. The entrance of the young Cuchulain, the putative hero, is delayed until this sense of desolation is irrevocably established. Unlike Cuchulain's similarly placed entrance in *The Green Helmet*, this entrance effects no lasting change in the play's mood. The audience's sense of Cuchulain's confidence and optimism is diminished by the old man's irritable garrulity, and by the unrelenting presence of the silent Guardian. His quest for the magic well seems doomed even before he articulates it.

The dramatist's simple decision to delay the exposition brings about a transformation in the audience's sense of the play's events. Not until the "eye of the mind" (CPL 136) has been made to see the well in all its bleakness do Cuchulain and the old man, in uneasy, tense conversation, reveal the well's properties and their reasons for having journeyed to it. As this expository conversation is completed, the play's immediate action commences. The Guardian, silent till now, gives the cry of a hawk. Cuchulain and the audience learn at the same time of the Guardian's complex multiple nature—part woman, part bird of prey, part unappeasable shadow.

One of the most effective dramatic strategies in the dance plays is to use the musicians to evoke a setting and mood rather than, as in the earlier *Deirdre*, to narrate the events that precede the beginning of the action. The narrative exposition instead becomes a part of the dialogue that follows the opening lyric and must, as in *At the Hawk's Well*, be measured against it. Thus, in Yeats's next dance play, *The Dreaming of the Bones*, the young revolutionary's plea for the strangers' help follows the opening lyric with its evocation of nameless shadows and the dreams of the dead. The central conflict in each of the dance plays is dramatically figured forth in the juxtaposition of the opening song, with its conjuration of mood and idea, and the opening moments of dialogue, with their setting forth of the play's essential circumstances. The dialogue, the dances, the lyrics rise out of the central idea. In this most lyric of dramatic forms, the playwright cleaves to the "mathematics" of dramatic logic.

The Only Jealousy of Emer completed 1919; performed 1926

A driving idea of the labor and pain with which human beauty must be achieved is implicit in the difficult opening lyric and the strange circumstances of *The Only Jealousy of Emer*. Yeats again draws on a story in Gregory's collection that bears the same title, but he undertakes a far more extensive alteration of the prose narrative. The events of Gregory's story occur before, not after, Cuchulain's encounter with Aoife's son. Cuchulain is wooed by Fand, an amorous woman of the Sidhe, who puts a spell of insensibility upon him that lasts for a year. Emer nurses him in his illness. On recovering, he has a tryst with the Woman of the Sidhe on Baile's Strand. Emer, who has never been jealous of Cuchulain's mortal mistresses, comes to Baile's Strand and attacks Fand with a knife. Cuchulain chides her: "The spear in your shaking hand does not wound me, nor your weak thin knife, nor your vain gathered anger" (CM 219).

> "Let me be given up," said Fand. "It is better for me to be given up," said Emer. "Not so," said Fand. "It is I that will be given up in the end; it is I that have been in danger of it all this time." And great grief and trouble of mind came to Fand, because she was ashamed to be given up. (CM 220)

From this narrative that turns on a decision made by one of the Sidhe, Yeats fashions a tragedy of human choice and human loss.

The play's opening song figures forth the human agony inherent in the otherworldly action. Pertinent to the song is the notion that the human soul lives many lives, with each life being an advance over the previous one. Before attaining to beatitude, the soul is permitted one incarnation as an astonishingly beautiful woman. Thus beauty is the result of great toil in many lives.

> How many centuries spent
> The sedentary soul
> In toils of measurement
> Beyond eagle or mole?
>
> (CPL 183)

"Toil" is charged with the multiple meanings of "labor" "labyrinth" and "entrapping net." In the play, Cuchulain will be caught in the toils of Fand's insistent words and her golden tresses. It is Emer who must undo the "bonds no man can unbind," and the difficulty of that act may drag into being her loveliness. In the song, as in the play it precedes, human beauty is flung out of storm.

In shaping this play, the dramatist seizes from Gregory's narrative the details of Cuchulain's insensibility, his wooing by Fand, Emer's jealousy, her vain attempt to attack the woman of the Sidhe with a knife. He invents more than he derives from Gregory, and his inventions absolutely transfigure the story, even though its central events grow out of the rivalry between Fand and Emer. He so fuses his own invention with details of the existing story that he gives his new enacted story all the power and resonance of ancient legend. He is making a new myth, imparting to a new story the weight of tradition. In so doing, he gives the voices of his dramatis personae such power as might accrue to the persons of Sophocles, a plangency achieved by few characters on the modern stage.

Yeats's simplest invention is to place this story immediately after Cuchulain's fight with the sea. As the action of Yeats's play commences, Cuchulain is in a state of insensibility, as he is for much of Gregory's narrative. But his insensible state in the drama is the result not of enchantments visited on him by the amorous Fand, but of the tragic folly of his killing his son and then fighting the waves. This shift in the temporal placement within the vast body of Cuchulain legends signals the effects of the changes Yeats is making to the story. In Gregory's narrative, the mortals remain the playthings of the gods. Both Cuchulain and Emer are given drinks of forgetfulness, so that they will never recall their commerce with an immortal. By contrast, the play centers on the causes and consequences of human action. It begins with Cuchulain suffering the results of his own choices, and it ends with Emer's choice.

In the play as first published, the dramatist foregrounds the enmity between the nonhuman creatures Fand and Bricriu. The Woman of the Sidhe curses the maker of discord for spoiling her eternal amour: "You that have no living light, but dropped / From a last leprous crescent of the moon."[14] In this version as in Gregory's narrative, Cuchulain and Emer remain playthings of the gods. But in the play's final version, the dialogue between Fand and Bricriu is cut. Instead the play's human figures direct the action and suffer its consequences.

Emer's climactic choice constitutes the most substantial difference between Yeats's telling of the story and Gregory's. In Gregory's narrative, the story turns on Fand's action. For all her angry and grieving talk, even with her thwarted knife-thrust at Fand, Gregory's Emer in story is essentially a passive sufferer. She has no power to affect the action. In Yeats's play, the action depends wholly upon her choice. Though this play is full of nonhuman characters, it turns, as do most of the world's great tragedies, upon a choice made by an uncertain and suffering human character. Emer's decision has most to do with turning the story from distant legend to immediate theatrical event.

The choice is Emer's alone, and she is given no draught of oblivion to free her from the knowledge of her action. She makes her choice in complete tragic recognition of its consequences to her husband and to herself. In tearing her husband from the only lover of whom she can be jealous, Emer renounces him forever and consigns him to a lonely death.

> He'll never sit beside you at the hearth
> Or make old bones, but die of wounds and toil
> On some far shore or mountain, a strange woman
> Beside his mattress.
>
> (CPL 189)

Like most of the plays of Yeats's maturity, this play depicts the conflict between the human and the nonhuman. "One of the antagonists does not wear a shape known to the world or speak a mortal tongue."[15] But as in Yeats's other mature plays, the human characters make the tragic choices, and in so doing win through to a difficult tragic triumph over the nonhuman.

The human dimension of this otherworldly tragedy is underscored by the circumstance that Emer's final renunciation is prompted by remorse in Cuchulain and by imperfection in the seemingly perfect Woman of the Sidhe. Cuchulain's ghost compares this woman to the moon that

> complete at last
> With every labouring crescent past
> And lonely with extreme delight
> Flings out upon the fifteenth night.
>
> (CPL 191)

Yeats's metaphysical system places each human personality into its corresponding lunar phase. But, "There's no human life at the full or the dark" (CP 184). Being a creature of the full moon, Fand must represent an energy other than the energy of human life. However, as Fand tells Cuchulain: "Because I long, I am not complete" (CPL 191). She is subject to human passion, love-longing, and this renders her incomplete. As Helen Vendler demonstrates, Yeats's metaphysical system provides him with a complex metaphor for the poetry of this play. Fand wants to kiss Cuchulain, for by this kiss she will be freed "from all the traces of primary tincture."[16] Whatever Fand is—immortal lover, muse, embodiment of the triumph of the imagination over daily circumstance—she is herself incomplete, and therefore vulnerable to Emer's power. Though Emer cannot reach her with a knife, Cuchulain's wife can break her inhuman rival's power by a very human act of jealousy.

And Emer is prompted to this act at last, not by Bricriu's mocking and goading, but by Cuchulain's speeches and acts of remorse. On the point of receiving Fand's kiss, Cuchulain turns away, recalls his marriage with Emer, and laments her loss. In the earlier version Cuchulain, unaided, gave up Fand. "Man is held to those whom he has loved / By pain they gave, or pain that he has given."[17] In the final version the husband and wife, from their different planes of being, act in concert. His remorse prompts her renunciation, and the relation with Fand is severed.

Out of his otherworldly materials, Yeats shapes a human tragedy. The play's cryptic final song, part celebration and mostly lament, sums up the action:

> He that has loved the best
> May turn from a statue
> His too human breast.
>
> (CPL 193)

In recalling Cuchulain to his human round and human destiny, Emer has lost him forever. Cuchulain, recalled to human toil, has lost that perfection and completeness for which the imagination most hungers. Given no draught of oblivion, both human protagonists will remember the bitter reward of tragedy.

The Words Upon the Window Pane first performed 1930

The play's action presents Cuchulain, hovering between life and death, engaged in a "dreaming back." A similar state is depicted in the spirit of Jonathan Swift, possessing the body of the trance medium Mrs. Henderson, in *The Words Upon the Window Pane*. In this play, first performed at the Abbey a year after the surprisingly successful Abbey performance of the prose version of *The Only Jealousy of Emer*, Yeats adopts all the conventional apparatus of plot and character from which he had labored to free himself in the plays for dancers. It is almost as if, having conquered the Abbey audience with a popularization of his strange dramaturgy of mask, dance, and the eerie conflict among mortals and immortals, he is now determined to conquer his audience once again by fusing his strange subjects with conventional dramatic structure. As Bradford, Clark and others have shown, Yeats adopts Ibsen's middle period dramaturgy for this play: prose dialogue, exposition through conversation, a realistic interior, an action rising by degrees to climax, familiar and recognizable characters, each depicted by a few precisely selected traits.[18] Set in the drawing-room of a Dublin lodging-house that two centuries before had been inhabited by the old and sick Jonathan Swift, the play depicts a seance in which Swift's raging spirit takes possession of a trance medium.

The employment of realistic dramaturgy might have afforded Yeats, as Bradford points out, a similar wry amusement as Shakespeare is supposed to have felt in making *The Tempest* conform to the unities. Yeats was certainly not above relishing confounding his critics. But the realistic form suits this play as no unrealistic form would. Swift's voice requires prose. Yeats was haunted by Swift's voice, his cadences, his distinct prose rhythms, and the dramatist captures them in the play. Nor can one imagine Swift dancing, as Cuchulain or Dervorgilla dance. His actions, like his speech, must be those he might realistically be supposed to have taken. Swift, after all, is a known historical figure, not a figure out of legend, and what is known about him sets limits on the manner in which he may be credibly portrayed. Samuel Beckett, Yeats's fellow countryman and arguably his heir in the ways of unrealistic drama, faced similar limitations when he set out to write an uncharacteristically realistic play about Samuel Johnson. While Yeats's evolving idea of tragedy required separating strangeness, a credible play about Swift required realistic dramaturgy. A realistic portrayal of a seance exactly suited all the playwright's purposes, and it had the added attraction of permitting him to fuse his lifelong passion for dialogues with the dead with his burgeoning passion for Swift.

While the contrasts between this sort of play and the dance plays with their varied verse forms, their stripping away of conventional exposition, and all their devices of separating strangeness are immediately apparent, one can discern striking though less apparent similarities between the dramaturgy of *The Words Upon the Window Pane* and the dramaturgy of the dance plays. Yeats gives this play a locale that resonates with an undead past. A characteristic of his new form of drama that he most prized was the ability to celebrate the rich history and ambience of each play's locale. The ghosts of generations of contending armies seem to float over the ruined abbey of Corcomroe, while the arid place of the dry well imprisons the blighted hopes of all those who have yearned for its plashing waters. Yeats lingers in these plays, far more than is usually possible in realistic drama, over what he considers to be sacred places. The interior where the action of *The Words Upon the Window Pane* takes place is similarly haunted by Swift's presence, even before that presence makes its most startling manifestation.

In its climactic scenes, the play bears a striking affinity to the dance plays. A separating strangeness quite as effective as the masked dance is achieved by virtue of the fact that Swift, Vanessa, and Stella inhabit a single medium's body. A single performer must employ gesture, tone of voice, manner, and action for the impassioned moralist and the two women who love him. Effects of separating strangeness are achieved by the fact of the seance itself. No role in Yeats, perhaps in modern drama, demands more of the performer. But in performance the scenes with Swift, Vanessa, and Stella, all contending within the body and speaking through the mouth of the medium, can be as riveting and startling, as tragically affecting, as anything in the dance plays.

Stella, of course, never speaks. It is deliberately unclear whether Swift is speaking directly to her or speaking in reverie to her image in his mind. Yet so powerfully is her presence evoked by his speech that, at the play's 1930 performance at the Abbey, spectators left the theater certain that they had actually seen and heard her.[19] No dramaturgical conjuration in the plays for dancers can be more effective than that.

In order fully to appreciate Swift's agony of passion and remorse, the audience must be taught a fair amount about spirits, seances, and the pertinent facts and circumstances of Swift's life. It is Yeats's dramaturgical task to impart a great deal of information about two difficult subjects without appearing to be either pedagogic or prolix. The task is all the harder because, as Bradford points out, Yeats tends to veer between excessive rapidity and excessive prolixity when he is discussing occult matters.[20]

As with *Deirdre*, composed nearly a quarter century earlier, the expository scenes gave Yeats most trouble. The exposition in its final form is driven by the simple, conventional device of creating a character who requires information. Corbett, a neophyte skeptic, knows as little as does the audience about the mechanics and culture of the seance room. In instructing him, Trench imparts the necessary information. But Yeats complicates Corbett by making this novice to spiritualism an expert on Swift. Even as Corbett receives instruction about trance mediumship, he is able to add to Trench's, and consequently the audience's, knowledge of Swift's life and circumstances.

Yeats punctuates the mutually instructive conversation with sequences that impart dramatic emphasis to what will emerge as the play's central idea. In one of these, Trench leads Corbett to the window pane and invites him to read the lines cut there. In a moment of astonished recognition, Corbett reads the lines aloud and identifies them as lines from Stella to Swift. Corbett's speaking the lines anticipates Swift's own expanded recitation of the same lines at the play's climax.

The lines themselves set forth one of the play's driving ideas: namely the continuous contrast of bodily with spiritual love. This idea receives many theatrical manifestations during the play—ranging from the terrible quarrel between Swift and Vanessa to the continuous contrast between Swift's arrogant intellect, as expressed in his noble prose, and Mrs. Henderson's startling description of the dirty, boil-covered old man. That Swift's words issue from the medium's unlikely mouth constitutes the most startling theatrical manifestation of the continuing contrast between body and mind. The heart's luster and the fading eyes in Stella's lines make for a first succinct statement of this recurring contrast.

Corbett's recognition of these lines prompts him to talk about Swift's intellect and his dread of the "ruin to come" (CPL 379). In one of the play's most effective dramatic juxtapositions, Corbett's speech is immediately followed by the entrance of the other spiritualists, with their talk of teashops, evangelists, and exorcisms. This sequence illustrates the leveling wind, the bourgeois concerns that, for Swift, exemplified the ruin he foresaw. The scene's dramatic devices, simple and effective, are deliberately similar to the dramatic devices Yeats employs for the climactic scenes with Swift. Corbett's surprised recognition of Stella's lines anticipates in tone and content Swift's terrible *anagnorisis*. The deliberate juxtaposition of Swift's epitaph with the petty ambitions and gripes of the seance-goers anticipates the juxtaposition of Swift's transcendent hope and dread with Vanessa's desire to add to the "healthy rascaldom and knavery of the world" (CPL 384). At once offsetting and enriching the necessary expository conversation, this sequence insures that, by the time Swift takes possession of the medium, the audience will know enough about seances and about Swift's life and passions, and it will also have a firm grasp on the play's driving ideas.

The persons whose passion brings the play to its climax, Swift, Vanessa, and Stella, do not appear at all during the exposition. Though Yeats is using a realistic mode, the device of the seance permits him to catch the characters that interest him at precisely the moment at which they interest him. The play has two distinct sets of characters—one set for the exposition, and one set for the tragic climax. Not even in the dance plays with their unconventional expositions had Yeats achieved so complete a separation between expository characters and tragic personalities. The device of the seance makes such separation the most natural means of shaping this particular play. This complete separation of the expository characters from the climactic persons—unique in drama—perfectly fits Yeats's strengths and weaknesses as a playwright.

The extant drafts of the play suggest that Yeats had a good deal less trouble with the scenes with Swift, Vanessa, and Stella than he did with the expository passages. Bradford does note that Yeats may have worked on the play in other drafts that do not survive, but on the available evidence, he seems to have known from the beginning of his work on the play what he wanted with these scenes.[21] This is all the more likely in that these scenes precisely conform to Yeats's idea of tragedy: passion defined by motives.

Swift's motives are revealed in this scene as desire for Vanessa and an opposing dread of begetting children: "I have something in my blood that no child must inherit" (CPL 383). Yet Swift is drawn to Vanessa in spite of himself. In performance, the medium's hands and arms must seem to take on a life of their own.

> It is not my hands that draw you back. My hands are weak. They could not draw you back if you did not love as I love. (CPL 384)

The sequence climaxes in Swift's frenzy of rage. Rising from her chair, the medium beats on the locked door.

> My God! Am I left alone with my enemy? Who locked the door? Who locked me in with my enemy? (CPL 384)

The "enemy" with whom Swift is confined is at once the persuasive, amorous woman, and his own terrible desire. Of course, Swift and his enemy inhabit the same medium's body whose fists are beating on the door. It is a fine irony that this climax resembles the scene from Galsworthy's *Justice* that Yeats had disparaged, remarking that anyone could beat on a door in the dark. He has arranged his scene in such a way that only the medium, possessed by Swift and Vanessa, can beat on this door in this way, and speak these words. In a theatrical sequence of absolute mastery, Yeats fuses the hated realism of the conventional theater with his own separating strangeness.

Were this a conventionally realistic play, the dramatist would need either to end it here, at this most intense moment of tragic conflict, or create a scene of credible transition that somehow moved his protagonist beyond rage, grief, and terror. Were Swift a character in a naturalistic Strindberg play—and he does, at times, resemble such characters—he might die of apoplexy, his heart cracked by fury, as does the Captain in *The Father*. Here again, the playwright is well served by his chosen form. In his play, it is not Swift himself who is caught in tragic rage, but Swift's unseen spirit possessing Mrs. Henderson's body. Thus the most credible transition is also the simplest. Swift's spirit leaves the medium to be replaced by her control, the fearful, poignantly wise spirit-child. "Bad old man does not know he is dead" (CPL 384). This line sums up Swift's situation with admirable concision. Her lines, together with the homely hymn she urges the spiritualists to sing, effect a credible dramatic modulation. "Did you notice the change while we were singing? The new influence in the room?" (CPL 385)

When Swift's spirit returns to the medium's body, his mood and circumstances are fundamentally altered. Trench's speeches have made the audience understand that spirits can pass with the rapidity of thought from one moment of their lives to another. Thus there need be no logical explanation, as there would have to be in a realistic play, for this change. Swift is engaged in precisely the sort of reverie that Yeats most admired in drama, that lifts its speaker quite out of ordinary facts and circumstances to where "passion, living through its thousand purgatorial years, as in the wink of an eye, becomes wisdom" (E and I 239). As do all tragic reveries, this one takes a specific circumstance as its point of departure. Swift asks Stella, and by extension himself, whether he has wronged her in depriving her of children, husband, and lover, in giving her only "a cross and aging man for friend; nothing but that" (CPL 385). That he is able to ask these questions in this tone—the prose rhythms of the speech require a quiet, adagio, lyric delivery—suggest how far he has moved beyond the rage and terror that these same considerations had excited in his scene with Vanessa. One source of this speech's resonance and force is its speaker's revealed ability to bring all the power of his intellect, his moral nature, to bear on questions which had, in the scene with Vanessa, reduced him to near bestiality. It is the words upon the window pane that enable him to perceive the intellectual and moral radiance of a relationship that embodies such ideal order and serenity as Corbett had described in the expository speeches. The medium's recitation of Stella's lines in Swift's voice takes on tremendous power for an audience that is hearing these words spoken for the second time under altered circumstances. Like a repeated refrain in one of Yeats's own lyric poems—"the solid man and the coxcomb"—the words upon the window pane accrue power as their meaning subtly changes.

> You taught how I might youth prolong
> By knowing what is right and wrong;
> How from my heart to bring supplies
> Of lustre to my fading eyes.
>
> (CPL 386)

In this prose drama that owes so much to a dramaturgy the playwright had shunned for most of his career, he ironically achieves one of his most effective tragic reveries, whose power derives from a careful shaping of the action. The reverie elicits tragic terror arising from the audience's knowledge, imparted in the play's early speeches, that Swift would indeed realize his most terrible fear—that he would outlive his friends and himself, that his unquiet spirit was destined to rage through the centuries. The very fact that Swift is speaking these serene words through a medium's mouth makes for a continuous counterpoint between the order to which he aspires and the subsequent ruin both of his life and his idea of civilization. The play's final moments reinforce this contrast. The Swift who continues to haunt the medium after the seance-goers have gone is the raging, life-hating Swift entrapped in a terrible solitude.

Using the known facts and circumstances of Swift's life, as he had earlier used Augusta Gregory's legends of the Red Branch, Yeats shaped in *The Words Upon the Window Pane* a tragedy whose soul is indeed its plot; from the strength of the plot, the characters, dialogue, and thought derive their power. So compelling is the playwright's shaped action that Yeats, limiting himself to prose and resorting at a climactic moment to the most brutal realism of having an actor beat upon a door, paradoxically achieves an apotheosis of tragic lyricism.

Purgatory first performed 1938

The Words Upon the Window Pane might have been a worthy swansong for Yeats the playwright. When his *Collected Plays* were published in

1934, this was the final play in the volume, a fitting capstone to a theatrical career that had begun forty years earlier with the 1894 production in London's Avenue Theatre of *The Land of Heart's Desire*. Yet it was a paradoxical capstone—a realistic prose play by a poet who aimed at tragic ecstasy. It remained for Yeats, at the end of his life, to make in *Purgatory* a play in verse that demonstrated a like mastery over dramatic action. Speaking two years after the play's first performance and a year after the playwright's death, T. S. Eliot, despite grave reservations over doctrine, singled out this play as Yeats's dramatic masterpiece. Eliot, himself in the process of mastering verse drama, described Yeats's achievement in words apposite to this late play.

> What is necessary is a beauty which shall not be in the line or the isolable passage, but woven into the dramatic texture itself; so that you can hardly say whether the lines give grandeur to the drama, or whether it is the drama which turns the words into poetry.[22]

Like that of *The Words Upon the Window Pane*, the immediate action of *Purgatory* is realistic. The tragedy does not turn, as in *The Dreaming of the Bones* and *The Words upon the Window Pane* upon the passion and remorse of spirits; rather it turns, as in *Ghosts* and *Rosmersholm* on the effect the passion of the dead has upon those who survive.

This short play's action develops with the simplicity, swiftness, and brutality of one of Yeats's late ballads. Two people, an old peddler and his illegitimate son, come to a ruined house. The peddler tells the boy the house's story, which is at once his own, in impassioned fragments. His mother, the scion of a noble family, had entered into a misalliance with a drunken groom. The old man views their sexual union, in which he was conceived, as the beginning and source of the ruin of the house and family. His putative motive in revisiting the ruined house is to release his mother's unquiet ghost from remorse. The old man's manner of telling the story, veering between elegiac reverence for a gracious, ordered past and unmitigable rage at a base, chaotic present, reveals the fault lines in his nature. In his conjuring the grand house and all its glorious history while the boy and the spectators see only an image of decay, the old man seems to move among the ghosts he beholds—to become himself a hungry and angry ghost patched with history. His articulated sense of nobility is at constant war with his propensity to enact the violence and chaos he professes to hate. In the midst of his fitful narrative to his son, he reveals that, long years ago, he has stabbed his father and burned the house. Now, witnessed only by the unresponsive ghost of his previous victim, he kills his son. "My father and my son on the same jackknife" (CPL 435).

The father's murder of his son is the only violent act in all Yeats's plays that occurs onstage. His plays are full of killing but, like the killing in Greek and French tragedy, his other killings happen offstage, out of the audience's sight. (Cuchulain is on stage when he is decapitated, but the stage darkens, so the audience never beholds the act of killing.) Seeing the old man stab his son to death convinces the spectators as no words could do that this is a polluted, evil figure, for all his talk of aristocratic order. *Purgatory*'s tragic irony springs from the fact that the old man is himself a chief part of the evil he seeks to eradicate. So long as he remains alive and active, the evil consequences of his mother's wedding night will continue, and his mother's spirit will be driven by remorse to relive her passion and to experience the full knowledge of its consequences.

An even more striking irony, apparently intentional on the playwright's part, is that the audience comes to know this protagonist far better than he knows himself. Throughout his dramatic career, Yeats had aimed to give life and form to transcendent moments of passionate perception. In the tragic reveries whose power he most often cites, Deirdre and her kin recognize their own lives' meaning and significance. They know at last and completely their own natures, and it is this hard-won self-knowledge that drives such persons to the tragic ecstasy Yeats so admired. Paradoxically, he chooses to shape the action of what may be his best play so as to diminish his protagonist's perception of his life's pattern and meaning. This wild old wicked man is not of the visionary company of Hamlet, Antony, and Deirdre.

In the play's earliest drafts, the old man knows full well from the outset that he is a part of the evil he is combating. He is returning to his ruined ancestral house with the express purpose of expunging that evil by killing his son. His sentiments in an early speech resemble those of Oedipus in his final moments, fully cognizant of the curse he carries. But where Oedipus's knowledge is the final result of his tragedy, the old man's knowledge is a mere given of the story.

> I that am the most evil of [?] them. This boy that is most evil still, . . . There is a dark evil, a curse that was never broke. . . . It begins; it corrupts man after man. . . . Accursed accursed—you and I accursed![23]

3 / RESHAPING THE PLOT

The old man realizes that he must kill his son, and his son allows himself to be killed almost as if he were a willing and knowing sacrifice.

> Come come come that I may kill and my mother find rest know that the evil is finished (boy rises and comes slowly to the old man—he strangles him.)[24]

The events of these early drafts—the misalliance between the aristocrat and the groom, the squandering of the estate, the burning of the house, the killing of the father, the mother's unquiet spirit, the killing of the son—are substantially the same as in the play's final form. The fundamental difference is in the old man's perception of the events and of his part in them. As Sandra Siegel demonstrates in her splendid introduction to *Purgatory*'s assembled drafts and manuscripts, the playwright systematically decreases his protagonist's self-knowledge through successive revisions.

With the decrease in each subsequent draft in the character's self-knowledge comes a concomitant increase for the play as a whole. In the play's final form, the old man believes himself to be a savior, an instrument of purification, while the audience knows him to be the chief source of pollution. This very disparity between the audience's understanding of the old man and his understanding of himself helps create the tragic power that most spectators and readers find in *Purgatory*. But Yeats never chooses to bring his protagonist, as Sophocles brings Oedipus, to a full knowledge of himself. This is an unusual choice, especially given Yeats's admiration for those speeches of tragic ecstasy that arise from moments of passionate perception. Siegel argues cogently that the old man's ignorance of his own abomination does not permit him to rise to the tragic ecstasy that, for Yeats, was the final excellence of drama. "*Purgatory* cannot be said to contain any joyful moments resembling those Yeats praises in other plays in the last sections of 'on the Boiler'."[25]

In the play's final version, there is one memorable sequence in which the old man approaches tragic joy—and then loses it. This is his vision of a purified soul, an event clearly central to a play called *Purgatory*. Other than the diminution of the old man's self-knowledge, the playwright's most substantial reshaping of the play's action concerns the quality of this vision. In the early drafts, as we have seen, the old man enters the action with a full consciousness of his own evil. After such knowledge, what forgiveness? Burdened by this knowledge, he immediately makes note of the house set in shadow, and the one riven tree, set in contrastingly bright moonlight.

> I hate that tree
> It is glittering white like something that has been
> Purified of its sins, like a soul that has passed
> From purgatory.[26]

As he revises the play, Yeats deliberately alters this disposition of events. The old man in the reshaped play is able to delude himself with the belief that, by killing his son, he can release his mother's soul from its dream. In the play's final version, the vision of the tree as purified soul comes not near the beginning, but near the end, as a seeming consequence of the old man's act. The transposition of this sequence brings about an enormous increase in dramatic power. The old man, instead of hating the tree for reminding him of a purified soul, can exalt—believing himself to have brought about the purgation the tree symbolizes. The speech becomes an evanescent moment of dramatic discovery and revelation. Remaining deluded, the old man never reaches full understanding of his responsibility for his mother's soul's continuing remorse. Even so, he briefly mounts to ecstasy in the play's final moment.

> Study that tree.
> It stands there like a purified soul—
> All cold, sweet, glistening light.
> Dear mother, the window is dark again,
> But you are in the light because
> I finished all that consequence.
>
> (CPL 435)

The old man's evanescent vision of light and purification is crushed beneath the inevitable pounding of the ghostly hoofbeats, and the play ends with his final despairing prayer.

Purgatory remains for many reasons a deeply disturbing play—in spite or perhaps because of its mastery of its form. Eliot regretted that, with its title, it offered "no hint or at least no emphasis upon purgation."[27] A play whose action turns on themes of class hatred and racial pollution is disturbing at any time, but one composed and first performed in 1938, while the Nazis were already putting their theories of racial purity into practice, must be especially disturbing. *Purgatory* is finally disturbing because it diverges, apparently quite deliberately, from Yeats's own ideal of tragedy. Lacking completeness of knowledge or vision, the old man's communicated experience of tragic ecstasy must be evanescent, ultimately false, and must give way to final despair. The effect is powerful, but tragic in a far different sense than that which Yeats describes in his discursive essays. Peter Ure describes the old man as being in a state of "crazy half-knowledge."[28] But can a deluded figure forever ignorant of himself and blind to his own deepest nature exist at the center of a tragedy? While terrible and complete self-recognition is a fundamental element in classical tragedy, it grows less pertinent to modern tragedy. The motives of persons on the modern stage grow ever more complex and obscure. The best-known characters in modern drama are not fully known to themselves. Mrs. Alving, in a play Yeats disliked, resembles Yeats's old man in that she never fully recognizes that she herself is the chief of the ghosts among whom she moves.

Though Yeats praised classical tragedy, he produced in *The Words Upon the Window Pane* and in *Purgatory* tragedies that lean closer to Ibsen than to Sophocles. The Ibsen on whom Yeats draws is not the theater poet who composed *Brand* or *Emperor and Galilean* or even the symbolist who produced *When We Dead Awaken*. Yeats is drawing instead on the dramaturgy of *Rosmersholm* and the other prose plays, each set in and around its haunted interior. Yeats the theorist and theater manager was at war with Ibsen all his life, decrying the Norwegian's meager language and bourgeois trappings. He likened Ibsen's characters to whimpering puppets, and wondered what law they had broken "that they had to wander round that narrow circle all their lives" (EXP 168–69). But in his latest and arguably most successful plays, it is to Ibsen that Yeats the playwright paradoxically turned.

Yeats's friend the great critic Arthur Symons had recognized, more than forty years before *Purgatory* was first produced and the year before *When We Dead Awaken*, that both poet-dramatists, for all their apparent differences, were engaged in the symbolist enterprise.

> Your own Irish literary movement is one of its expressions; your own poetry and A. E.'s poetry belong to it in the most intimate sense. In Germany it seems to be permeating the whole of literature. Its spirit is that which is deepest in Ibsen.[29]

Yeats and Ibsen were both seeking ways to give indirect expression to those half-known, half-uttered things that could find expression in no other way. For both *The Words Upon the Window Pane* and *Purgatory*, Yeats chose Ibsen's favorite setting: a house distorted by a tragic history whose ghosts impinge upon the buried lives of its present inhabitants. *Purgatory*'s terrible beauty springs in part, as does *Hedda Gabler*'s terrible beauty, from the spectators' sense of depths within a character that the character half-senses, but cannot know or express.

The Yeats-Ibsen juxtaposition is a difficult one. On the surface, no two figures in modern theater seem less alike. But in reading Eric Bentley's classic description of Ibsen's achievement as a playwright, one might just as easily be reading a description of *Purgatory*.

> The ballad is indeed the nearest thing to an Ibsen play in all earlier literature. A ballad celebrates a recent disaster. An air of fatality broods over it. It is compressed. It is all catastrophe. Upon such a mythic pattern Ibsen built a naturalistic superstructure.[30]

Yeats scorned the naturalistic superstructure, but in *Purgatory* he put Ibsen's mythic pattern to his own uses. In its violent starkness, its brooding, its half-explained, half-known curse, *Purgatory* too resembles a ballad.

Always experimenting, always seeking means of keeping the impinging bourgeois world at a distance, Yeats circled at the end of his career toward the dramatist he had wrongly scorned as the quintessential bourgeois realist. Perhaps half-consciously, he detected at last the same profoundly symbolist elements in Ibsen that Symons had detected so many years earlier. In his last years, his mastery over the difficult shaping of dramatic action was such that he could use, without being subsumed by, the greatest modern maker of dramatic action. He took that which was deepest in Ibsen and fused it with that which was deepest in himself. In so doing he created, in two plays composed during his last decade, a shaped and reshaped form of drama that was wholly and peculiarly his own.

4
Opinions and Ideas

For meditations upon unknown thought
Make human intercourse grow less and less.
—*"All Souls' Night"*

In *Reveries Over Childhood and Youth* Yeats recalled a practice of his father's that exerted a lasting influence over the future dramatist's ideal in making plays.

> At breakfast he read passages from the poets, and always from the play or poem at its most passionate moment. He never read me a passage because of its speculative interest, and indeed did not care at all for poetry where there was a generalisation or abstraction however impassioned. (AU 42)

Yeats absorbed and assimilated his father's distrust of speculation and abstraction in poetry. The words "logic," "generalization," and "opinion" bear increasingly negative associations in his writing. His hours spent in political meetings listening to shrill voices utter abstract opinions created in him the settled conviction, rooted in his own experience, that the abstract intellect is in perpetual opposition to rich, variegated life. "An error of the group is to continually mistake a philosophical idea for a spiritual experience" (MEM 149).

Yeats drew a fundamental distinction between opinion and conviction. While opinion was based on abstract speculation, conviction derived from engagement with experience. He always measured his hatred of abstract opinions by his sense of how these had blighted Maud Gonne's life.

> Have I not seen the loveliest woman born
> Out of the mouth of plenty's horn,
> Because of her opinionated mind
> Barter that horn and every good
> By quiet natures understood
> For an old bellows full of angry wind?
>
> (CP 113)

Thinking of Maud Gonne, he wrote in his journal that women "give themselves to an opinion as if it were some terrible stone doll.... At last the opinion becomes so much a part of them that it is as though a part of their flesh becomes, as it were, stone, and much of their being passes out of life." (MEM 192)

The playwright was sensitive to the charge that his own plays were expressions of opinion. In notes written for Horace Plunkett's use in the inquiry of 1904 into the Abbey Theatre's patent he vigorously defended himself against the British charge that *Cathleen ni Houlihan* had been a piece of propaganda:

> It may be said that it is a political play of a propagandist kind. This I deny. I took a piece of human life, thoughts that men had felt, hopes they had died for, and I put this into what I believe to be a sincere dramatic form. I have never written a play to advocate any kind of opinion, and I think that such a play would be necessarily bad art, or at any rate a very humble kind of art.[1]

While abstract opinion for Yeats had the Medusa effect of turning a living thing to stone, "thoughts that men have felt," growing out of experience, could be equated with human life. His writing and rewriting of philosophical plays was a perpetual struggle to transform opinion into felt thought.

> God guard me from those thoughts men think
> In the mind alone;
> He that sings a lasting song
> Thinks in a marrow-bone.
>
> (CP 326)

Yet the shrillness of Yeats's letter to Plunkett suggests that the British charge that he was writing propagandist plays touched a nerve. By the time he wrote this letter, he had become deeply embroiled in continuing public controversy. On behalf of his vision of the Irish Theatre, and often in fierce opposition to his fellow theater artists, he engaged in polemic, theory, generalization, propaganda.

Yeats's distrust of opinion was matched by an equally fierce advocacy. He clung to opinions about the invisible world, or about the poet's proper place in society, sometimes as tightly as did the hysterical women he aspersed. Although he insisted repeatedly on his distrust of philosophy in drama, he gave over a significant portion of his creative life to making and remaking philosophical plays which did indeed advocate their author's opinions. During the early years of the Irish National Theatre, his opinions leached much life from some of his plays.

He produced two such plays *Where There is Nothing* 1902—composed, so he claimed later, in two weeks with help from Augusta Gregory and Douglas Hyde—and *The Hourglass* 1903. Neither play satisfied him. *The Hourglass* made him ashamed, and he withdrew *Where There is Nothing* from his collected works. But he kept revising these plays for many years. That the playwright did not simply jettison them is strong evidence of his own growing conflict about philosophical drama.

For Aristotle, thought remained one of the drama's constituent elements, and he declared it as one of only two natural causes from which actions spring.[2] Thought, as a dramatic element, is prominent in *The King's Threshold, The Player Queen, The Resurrection, The Death of Cuchulain*. One must set these plays and the years of labor Yeats gave them against his repeated theoretical pronouncements against philosophy in the theater. For all his professed delight in active men, he was drawn again and again to central figures, from Paul Rutledge to the nameless young men in *The Resurrection*, who were driven quite as much as the protagonists of the admired and hated Shaw by their ideas. The effort he gave to these plays suggests his unwilling recognition that thought, even though it might trouble the living stream of his plays, was quite as necessary to that life as was action.

The Hourglass first performed 1903; revised 1911–12; 1914

The nameless hero of *The Hourglass*, referred to with simple irony as the Wise Man, is driven by the idea, anathema to the playwright, that only the visible world exists. The play's conflict of ideas arises when an angel, upon whose impossibility the Wise Man had insisted, appears with a message that the Wise Man will die when the sands in his hourglass run down, and that his soul, whose existence he had also denied, will be perpetually damned unless he can find someone who believes in the invisible worlds of Heaven, Purgatory, and Hell. The Wise Man pleads that he had denied the existence of Hell, and the Angel responds that "Hell is the place of those who deny" (VPL 600). The Wise Man is terrified into espousing religious belief: "I will say to them that only amid spiritual terror or only when all that laid hold on life is shaken can we see truth" (VPL 622).

In this early essay in philosophical drama, Yeats uses the simplest means of having his characters express thoughts. His central character spends most of the play engaged either in soliloquy or argument. There is relatively little action other than heated conversation—the sort of thing Yeats would come to describe pejoratively as "rhetoric." From the outset, the nameless hero is no more than the mouthpiece of an idea. Indeed Yeats seems to have conceived his protagonist as a crude parody of the materialists he himself had been fighting throughout the nineties. Driven by newly discovered spiritual terror to repudiate his materialism, the Wise Man kneels to the Fool and begs for salvation. The Fool's refusal to say the necessary words of belief brings the Wise Man to his final insight. "We sink in on God, we find Him in becoming nothing—we perish into reality" (VPL 634). This is close to an insight reached by Paul Rutledge, one of Yeats's other early philosophical protagonists: "Where there is nothing there is God" (VPL 1164). Yeats would hold to this idea through many vicissitudes and give it memorable expression in a late sonnet that dramatically contradicts many of his earlier assertions about the opposition of philosophy to life.

> but man's life is thought
> And he, despite his terror, cannot cease
> Ravening through century after century,
> Ravening, raging, and uprooting that he may come
> Into the desolation of reality.
>
> (CP 333)

Brought to reality through terror, the Wise Man knows at last that he will not be saved.

Be silent. May God's will prevail though that be my damnation! What was I born for but that I might cry that His will be fulfilled upon the instant, though that be my damnation? (VPL 636)

None of the spoken words made so strong an impression on the play's first audiences as the spectacle of the Wise Man kneeling to the Fool. As produced in 1903, *The Hourglass* was a simple parable of religious conversion and as such it remained popular in the repertoire of the burgeoning Irish National Theatre. Yeats's unease about the play is suggested by the variant contradictory notes he published with it.

> I was faintly pleased when I converted a music-hall singer and kept him going to Mass for six weeks, so little responsibility does one feel for that mythological world, but I was always ashamed when I saw any friend of my own in the theater. (VPL 646)

> [I] tried to put my own philosophy into the words. An action on the stage, however, is so much stronger than a word that when the Wise Man abused himself before the Fool I was always ashamed. My own meanings had vanished and I saw before me a cowardly person who seemed to cry out "the wisdom of this world is foolishness" and to understand the words not as may a scholar and a gentleman but as do ignorant preachers. (VPL 645–46)

That Yeats chose to revise the play several times over the years between 1911 and 1922 suggests that his notions about the relations between drama and philosophy, for all his theoretical pronouncements, remained fluid and troubled. One stimulus to revise the play was Nugent Monck's coming to the Abbey as director in 1911. Monck was interested in medieval drama, and during his tenure he chose to revive Yeats's early plays with their trappings of medieval morality. Theatrical exigency may have dovetailed with the playwright's deeper need to return to this play between 1911 and 1914. Examination of Yeats's writing during these years in which, as Bradford argues, he became a great writer, suggests that the central idea of *The Hourglass* had indeed become part of his fundamental thought and art.

Several revisions in the 1914 verse version are worth glancing at because of what they reveal about the playwright's continuing attempts to find adequate dramatic expression for complex ideas that he did not wish to cheapen. In the 1903 version, the Wise Man simply turns in his book to the passage about the invisible country. For the revision, Yeats invents a scene with the pupils and the Fool prior to the Wise Man's initial entrance.

> **2 PUPIL** Let us choose a subject by chance. Here is his big book. Let us turn over the pages slowly. Let one of us put down his finger without looking. The passage his finger lights on will be the subject for the lesson. . . .
> **4 PUPIL** Spread it on Teigue's back, and then we can all stand round and see the choice.
>
> (VPL 579–81)

The book spread out on the fool's back with the pupils choosing a passage at random is a perfect emblem of the operations of that invisible world the Wise Man denies. In the revised play's opening moments, the fool seems to become the agent of that world. Through the apparent operations of chance, the invisible country is forcing itself on the Wise Man's notice.

In its 1903 version, *The Hourglass* had depicted a simple conflict between an atheist and received religion. The Wise Man's greatest triumph had been his victory over a monk, which had resulted in the abolition of religious observance. In bringing the play closer to his own thought, the playwright excised such words as "soul," "Heaven," "blessed," and "God." Two such changes occur at the beginning and the end of the central scene between the Wise Man and the Angel. In the 1903 version, the Angel's first line is: "I am the Angel of the Most High God" (VPL 598). In the final verse version, the Wise Man is implicated from the outset in the Angel's embassage.

> **ANGEL** I am the crafty one that you have called.
> **WISE MAN** How that I called?
> **ANGEL** I am the messenger.
>
> (VPL 599)

When the angel leaves the stage in the 1903 version, the Wise Man proclaims the full force of his conversion. "Blessed be the Father, blessed be the Son, blessed be the Spirit, blessed be the Messenger They have sent" (VPL 606). The theological conflict is unequivocal, and God's victory is complete. In the 1914 verse version, the Wise Man is not given time to say anything. As the Angel is leaving, the pupils reenter, performing a dance of mockery around the Fool. Indeed, even as the Angel is giving her final adjuration, the pupils can be heard offstage singing a song to the Fool that applies to the Wise Man. "Who stole your wits away / And where are they gone?" (VPL 605) Excising the Wise Man's prayer that had appeared at this point in the play, Yeats invents a scene that uses the theater's resources of dance and song to create an impression that could not be created by discursive prose. The scene of satyrnalian revelry evokes the world beyond the senses the Wise Man had denied.

The moment in the early version that caused Yeats the greatest unease is the Wise Man's act of kneeling to the fool.

> No, no, I have not the courage. (He kneels.) Have pity upon me, Fool, and tell me! (VPL 632)

Yeats's first and simplest alteration is to cut the stage direction. He also changes the begging and self-pitying prose into verse whose tone is self-command and even self-conquest.

> Be silent. May God's will prevail on the instant,
> Although His will be my eternal pain.
> I have no question:
> It is enough, I know what fixed the station
> Of star and cloud.
> And knowing all, I cry
> That whatso God has willed
> On the instant be fulfilled,
> Though that be my damnation.
>
> (VPL 637)

The shortened lines and rhyming words intensify the Wise Man's thought and fix it in the minds of his hearers.

Altering the words and tone as well as the action of his protagonist, Yeats fashions a figure who achieves mastery over himself and exemplifies an observation the playwright had made in his journal a couple of years before remaking this play: "Men are dominated by self-conquest, and thought that is a little obvious, a little platitudinous if merely written, becomes persuasive, immortal even, when it has been held to amid the hurry of events. The self-conquest of the writer who is not a man of action is style" (MEM 212).

In the most dramatically successful passages of *The Hourglass*, the playwright used parable, metaphor, emblem, dance, to suggest ideas that are not readily available to sense and reason. He worked to create a language and action that could suggest the invisible, and to create characters who would credibly cling to what the symbols suggest. When the Wise Man dies, clinging to the faith that there are indeed things that we can neither see nor touch, the Fool gives him the appropriate epitaph. "You and I, we are the two fools, we know everything, but we will not speak" (VPL 639). In its final verse revision, the play is less about an idea than about the passion in and through which the idea has been created.

More than most poets, Yeats was given to philosophical generalization. The young James Joyce famously admonished him that the habit of generalization marked him not as a poet but a man of letters.[3] Yeats himself recognized that his discursive itch endangered his art: "I find that my philosophical tendency spoils my playwriting if I have not a separate channel for it" (L 533). At the same time philosophy freed him to write the plays that would have been inconceivable without it. But philosophical drama does not admit of separate channels for the expression of thought and the creation of art. In Yeats's philosophical plays, he labored with mixed results to make the expression of thought a living part of his art.

The King's Threshold first performed 1903; revised 1904, 1906, 1922

Thought at times fuses with art in *The King's Threshold*. The play's chief figure is driven by his certainty that poetry must have an important place in the governing of a nation. As Max Beerbohm observed of the play, Yeats had discovered that he was not taken seriously enough, and, "being Irish, demanded his due in a play rather than through writing letters to the papers or pompous articles."[4] Denied his proper place at the king's table, Seanchan the poet is starving himself upon the king's doorstep. The play's action springs from the various assaults the king and his allies mount against Seanchan's resolve.

One of the playwright's dramatic strategies is to devise scenes in which Seanchan, rather than expounding his ideas, elicits their articulation from his doubting pupils. In so doing, he forces their minds and spirits to discover or rediscover the truth of what their mouths are saying.

> **SEANCHAN** I bid that pupil tell me
> Why poetry is honored, wishing to know
> If he had any weighty argument
> For distant countries and strange churlish kings!
> What did he answer?
> **ELDEST PUPIL** I said that poets
> Hung images of the life that was in Eden
> About the childbed of the world, that it
> Looking upon those images might bear
> Triumphant children.
>
> (CPL 73)

This is one of the play's central tenets, and it gains in dramatic force by being uttered, under duress, by the pupil and not the master.

The protagonist of this philosophical play scorns discursive statement. Consequently, he gives life to his ideas by expressing them, or by forcing others to express them, in myth and metaphor. When the bumbling comic mayor appeals to him with the semblance of reason, he replies:

> Reason, o reason in plenty! Yet you have
> yellowy-white hair and not too many teeth.
> How comes it that you have been so long in the world
> And not found reason out?
>
> (CPL 77)

This savage response gives a clear signal that Seanchan will never reach after fact and reason in giving expression to the idea that drives him. Neither he nor anyone else in the play explains in discursive language why the poet's place among the lawgivers is worth dying for. The explanation resides in the play's many demonstrations of the power of poetry.

Poetry's Nietzschean power of joyful destruction is displayed by the rhythmically chanted curses called down on the Mayor by the old servant and the cripples. As in the pupils' dance around the Fool in *The Hourglass,* Yeats is using the theater's resources of rhythm and action to embody an idea:

> The curse of wrinkles be upon him. Wrinkles where his eyes are, wrinkles where his nose is, wrinkles where his mouth is, and a little old devil looking out of every wrinkle. (CPL 79)

In one of the play's most spectacular moments the protagonist, who has spent most of his stage time sitting or half reclining in physical weakness, rises in fury, condemns the food as leprous, and flings it about the stage. The flying food inevitably brings a farcical note into the scene, but the farce grows savage and serious as Seanchan utters his ominous threat.

> Be gone! or I will give my curse to you.
> You have the leper's blessing, but you think
> Maybe the bread will something lack in savor
> Unless you mix my curse into the dough.
>   (CPL 87)

Seanchan's insistent lines make leprosy a dominant, repeated image from here to the play's end. It joins with other images of physical deformity in mythic illustration of the notion, never discursively stated but implicit in the action and language, that the world in which poetry is no longer a revered participant is a world diseased, crooked, rotting from within.

When Seanchan's lover Fedelm becomes the last and most powerful voice in the growing chorus to persuade the poet to eat, he makes a Nietzschean myth of the genesis of an overmastering race.

> The stars had come so near me that I caught
> Their singing. It was praise of that great race
> That would be haughty, mirthful, and white-bodied
> With a high head and open hand; and how
> Laughing it would take the mastery of the world.
>   (CPL 89)

In Seanchan's developing mythos, white may be the color of the coming superman, as well as of disease. In a moment of dramatic ambiguity too rare in this play, the mastering race Seanchan heralds partakes of the very disease he decries.

Even at its best, the play is too simply and monotonously the dream's battle with reality. The antagonists are frozen in their respective philosophical positions. The playwright's strictures to the contrary, the life of his characters is choked off by their clinging too closely to ideas. The notion of the poet's rightful place in society, as Seanchan clings to it, resembles the troubling stone about which Yeats writes so ruefully in his journal and so tragically in "Easter, 1916." Emblematic of the play's fundamental problem is a scene that should be the dramatic climax. Seanchan is at the point of taking food from Fedelm. The stage direction is revealing: "(He takes bread from Fedelm, hesitates, and then thrusts it back into her hand.) But no! I must not eat it" (CPL 90). It is dramatically credible that the weakened poet should momentarily forget his resolve and take food from his lover. But the playwright does not make credible Seanchan's thrusting the food back at Fedelm. An inventive actor or director might find credible and even moving circumstances to prompt this action. Perhaps Seanchan's eyes light on one of his own poetic creations, or perhaps, from offstage, a harp played by one of his pupils might be heard. But there is no passionate moment of discovery leading to reversal in the scene as written. Yeats's creature, frozen into an idea, shows himself to be his author's puppet and not a living personality. Though Yeats's tone and intention are far from comic, his chief figure, locked by an unchanging set of beliefs into a predictable set of behaviors, resembles nothing so much as one of Henri Bergson's comic creatures in whom something mechanical has been encrusted upon a living organism.[5]

The play's structure suffers from similar problems. As originally produced, *The King's Threshold* had a happy ending in which the poet was restored to his rightful place at the king's table. In 1922, Yeats made a new tragic ending that gave Seanchan a glorious death. There is no better indication of the play's peculiar shortcomings than the fact that neither its tone nor Seanchan's character alters with the altered ending. In a prologue Yeats wrote for the original 1903 production, published in the *United Irishman* about a month before the first performance but never performed, he expressed what would prove a lasting uncertainty about the happy ending: "Some think it would be a finer tale if Seanchan had died at the end of it, and the king had the guilt at his door, for that might have served the poet's cause better in the end. But that is not true, for if he that is in the story but a shadow and an image of poetry had not risen up from the death that threatened him, the ending would not have been true and joyful enough to be put into the voices of players and proclaimed in the mouths of trumpets, and poetry would have been badly served" (VPL 313).

In all the revisions before 1922, the pupils' willingness to die with Seanchan forces the king to relent.

> Kneel down, kneel down! He has the greater power.
> There is no power but has its roots in his.
> I understand it now; there is no power
> But his, that can withhold the crown or give it;
> Or make it reverent in the eyes of men.[6]

Accompanied by a trumpet blast, the joyous pupils sing a Nietzschean paean to a better world, enriched for all time by the lawgiving poet.

> O silver trumpets, be you lifted up
> And cry to the great race that is to come.
> Long-throated swans upon the waves of time,
> Sing loudly, for beyond the wall of the world
> That race may hear our music and awake.
>   (VPL 311–12)

This speech, first added in 1906, intensifies and focuses the sense of joy and triumph, bringing to fuller life what had always been implicit in the play.[7]

The play's conclusion is an ecstatic celebration of Seanchan's strength of will and poetry's triumph. It is surprising how little the tone changes when, in 1922, Yeats writes a tragic ending. King Guaire, in this version, is not won over by the magnanimity of Seanchan's pupils. Seanchan, filled with renewed joy by their willingness to die with him, rises to praise them. In his weakened state, the act of rising is a triumphant gesture.

> I need no help.
> He needs no help that joy has lifted up
> Like some miraculous beast out of Ezekiel!
> The man that dies has the chief part in the story.
>   (CPL 93)

Though the play's joy is deepened and intensified by the sounding of the new tragic note, as well as by the fact that the Yeats of 1922 is a better writer than the Yeats of 1904 or 1906, the new ending's tone and philosophic thrust are almost identical to those of the old happy ending in which the king relents. Whether Seanchan is ascending to his rightful place in a restored world or to an exultant escape through death from a corrupted world, his is a happy triumph, appropriately accompanied by trumpets. The Nietzschean trumpet call to the "race that is to come" passes virtually unchanged from the old anastrophe to the new catastrophe. Events around Seanchan do not change him. His ecstasy can result as easily from his death as from his restoration. Stone-like, he clings to his idea of poetry and passes out of life.

In response to the youngest pupil's triumphant exhortation to the trumpets, the eldest pupil offers a more muted dirge.

> Not what it leaves behind it in the light
> But what it carries with it to the dark
> Exalts the soul. Nor song nor trumpet-blast
> Can call up races from the worsening world
> To mend the wrong and mar the solitude
> Of the great shade we follow to the tomb.
>
> (CPL 94)

This fleeting dialectic between Seanchan's two best pupils, the spokesman for poetic triumph and the spokesman for the world's diminishment, is the only genuine exploration this schematic, philosophical play affords of the changing relations between a worsening world and poetry. The Yeats of 1922 was searching a diminished world, and was discovering and exploring poetry's possible complicity in that diminishment. He was giving his poet's mind free play over difficult ideas in difficult poems like "Nineteen Hundred and Nineteen" and "Meditations in Time of Civil War," while he was not giving the mind of his creature Seanchan free play in the philosophical drama, even with its altered ending.

In later years Yeats grew increasingly impatient with the sort of drama whose chief aim was to espouse a point of view, whose characters were rendered inorganic by too close an identification with an author's opinions. Such impatience led to his controversial rejection of Sean O'Casey's *The Silver Tassie*. O'Casey had been the Abbey's most successful playwright of the twenties, and Yeats had defended him against adverse reaction to *The Plough and the Stars*.

Now O'Casey had submitted *The Silver Tassie,* a new play about the Great War, and Yeats believed that this play's thought froze its action. He took particular exception to the second act, in which nameless soldiers decry war's horror in ritual fashion. For Yeats, unmoved by O'Casey's striking use of theatrical resources such as the eerily silent flashes that end the act, the younger dramatist was committing the same sins that he himself had committed in his early philosophical plays. Writing to Olivia Shakespeare, he characterized O'Casey's play as "all anti-war propaganda to the exclusion of plot and character" (L 743). Yeats wrote O'Casey a letter in which he seemed as much to be quarreling with his earlier self as instructing the younger dramatist. While O'Casey would take Yeats's letter, point by point, as an antimodel and would continue to write plays precisely unlike those Yeats wanted him to write,[8] Yeats would, during his last decade of playwriting, closely adhere to the advice he was here giving:

> The only way poetry can be philosophical is by portraying the emotions of a soul dwelling in the presence of certain ideas. Among the things that dramatic action must burn up are the author's opinions. While he is writing, he has no business to know anything that is not a portion of the action. Do you suppose for one moment that Shakespeare educated Hamlet and King Lear by telling them what he thought and believed? As I see it, Hamlet and Lear educated Shakespeare, and I have no doubt that in the process of that education he found out that he was an altogether different man to what he thought himself and had altogether different beliefs. A dramatist can help his characters to educate him by thinking and studying everything that gives them the language they are groping for through his hands and eyes. But the control must be theirs; and that is why the ancient philosophers thought a poet or dramatist daemon-possessed. (L 741–2)

Unsympathetic to the sort of expressionistic political theater O'Casey was creating, Yeats perceived only an author turning his characters to stone by imposing his opinions upon them. Yeats's own increasing hatred of opinion that is born of abstraction and not of experience probably led him to misjudge O'Casey's achievement. Unsympathetic to the younger playwright's objectives, Yeats judged him to have abandoned his own lived experience for mere abstraction.

You were interested in the Irish Civil War, and at every moment of those plays wrote out of your own amusement with life or your sense of its tragedy. You were excited, and we all caught your excitement. You were exasperated almost beyond endurance by what you had seen or heard, as a man is by what happens under his window, and you moved us as Swift moves his contemporaries. But you are not interested in the Great War. You never stood on its battlefields or walked its hospitals; and so you write out your own opinions. You illustrated those opinions by a series of almost unrelated scenes, as you might in a leading article. (L 740–41)

Yeats's own hard experience had taught him the damage an author's opinions imposed on his characters can inflict on the life of his plays. But the playwright needed ideas and their discursive expression as much as he distrusted them. His early drafts, as Bradford demonstrates, were abstract and expository.[9] An entry in his journal suggests that ideas, rather than images or actions, may be at the very foundation of his acts of creation.

> In Christianity what was philosophy in Eastern Asia became life—biography, drama. A play passes through the same processes in being written. At first, if it has psychological depth, there is a bundle of ideas, something that can be stated in philosophical terms; my *Countess Cathleen*, for instance, was once the moral question, may a soul sacrifice itself for a good end?—but gradually philosophy is eliminated more and more until at last the only philosophy audible, if there is even that, is the mere expression of one character or another. When it is completely life it seems to the hasty reader a mere story. (MEM 150)

Perhaps Yeats was so vehement in accusing O'Casey of choking his characters' life with ideas not their own because he was forever battling a similar practice in himself. Hating abstract ideas, he yet recognized that they are "connected with poetry, or rather with passion—one half its life, and yet its enemy" (L 588).

In his early tutelary plays, Yeats was aiming to persuade his audience to adopt his opinions about the unseen world or about the poet's proper place in society. These opinions had become his own stone dolls. For his later plays, he began to distinguish between opinions and ideas. "We grow like others through opinions, but through ideas discover ourselves, for these are only true when images of our own power" (EXP 237). Yeats was developing a dramatic relation with the ideas that drove his plays. Rather than clinging to them as if they were stone dolls, he was playing with them, and allowing his characters to play with them, as if they were masks.

The Player Queen first performed 1919; revised 1922

Playing with ideas, he composed in *The Player Queen* a philosophical drama that was fully alive. The play describes a company of players who come to a nameless city wracked by political and metaphysical intrigue. The leading lady, putting on the queen's regalia, becomes the queen and sets in motion a new era. In "Per Amica Silentia Lunae" Yeats describes the idea out of which the play grew and notes his means of moving from idea to drama.

> Some years ago, I began to believe that our culture with its doctrine of sincerity and self-realisation made us gentle and passive, and that the Middle Ages and the Renaissance were right to found theirs upon the imitation of Christ, or of some classic hero. Saint Francis and Cesare Borgia made themselves overmastering, creative persons by turning from the mirror to meditation upon a mask. (M 333–34)

To illustrate the efficacy of putting ideas into action, the "real" queen in the finished play uses a mirror, while the Player Queen plays with a mask.

Yeats began to work on *The Player Queen* in 1907, intending it for Mrs. Patrick Campbell, who was to triumph as Deirdre in the following year. He kept at it off and on for years, neither publishing it nor attempting to have it produced. The play's many drafts demonstrate that its author had more than his usual difficulty getting beyond abstraction and exposition. Early versions of the play's characters expound as if they were philosophical essayists. In one of many debates, a cantankerous first minister tries to convince a timid queen to assume the mask of sovereignty. The queen's duty, he argues, is to make the people greater by what she seems. She is the image of what they would be:

> She can grant to others the government as you have granted it to me. She may sorrow for her sins, but she must always seem to be all power and haughtiness. Your state is a mask which you must wear always on your face.[10]

The Prime Minister and the unwilling queen make up one of two pairs of debaters in these early drafts. For the other pair, the topic of contention is also the mask. Yellow Martin, the sincere lover, a figure whose manner of clinging tightly to an opinion calls to mind Seanchan or Paul Rutledge is assailed by Peter, the light lover, the wearer of and player with masks.

> **PETER**   It is we light lovers who understand love. We make ourselves what a woman wishes.
> **YELLOW MARTIN**   But I wish her to be all the perfection I can imagine, and would be no less myself.
> **PETER**   Seem a little, play a little.[11]

Yeats was to chide O'Casey for not allowing his characters to instruct him as Peter does here. During his long labor, the author of *The Player Queen* seems to have been taking instruction from his characters as they evolved. From the Prime Minister, the light lover, and the player queen in their various avatars, Yeats learned a useful analogy between playing with masks and playing with ideas. Through ideas, as through masks, one can discover oneself and acquire power. In clinging hysterically to inflexible notions of sincerity, the romantic lover and the real queen, like the playwright who clings hysterically to opinions, vitiate their power and choke off their dramatic life.

But like teachers, all the characters in the play's early drafts lecture each other. What thwarted the playwright in draft after draft was a difficulty in making his persons reveal their thought dramatically, rather than simply state it. The playwright had to think out the ideas, then examine their implications in discursive language, before he could figure them forth in action. He used the early versions of these characters as vehicles for philosophic exploration, and though the exploration would serve him well both in this play and in much other work, he was too good a dramatist to declare the play complete. So exploring the related ideas of self and role, mask and face, he continued to work on draft after draft, year after year.

Yeats's theatrical and philosophical interests were centering on the mask during his years of work on *The Player Queen*. From the earliest drafts through its final version, the play features a company of performers who use masks. In early drafts the Prime Minister, assuming the role of acting coach for the Queen, seizes on the natural association. Picking up one of the players' masks, he says: "Could I find one of these that suited me, I'd be the king myself."¹² He goes on:

> a little wearing of the mask, that is all I will have of you. If you would win obedience, you must seem all the greatness your people dream of, all that they would be if they could.¹³

Though most of these speeches are winnowed away as the play moves toward final form, Yeats retains the central juxtaposition of the worlds of political and theatrical intrigue. Juggling these similar worlds, he fashions a story through which his evolving ideas can be revealed, rather than simply expounded.

During his many years of work on the play, Yeats was exploring the implications inherent in the assumption of a role or mask, and these explorations came to fruition in the completed play. In various drafts, he tried to invent actions embodying the idea that the mask can infuse both power and purpose into its wearer. In one draft, the leading player wears the real queen's regalia. Consequently the soldiers convince themselves that the Player Queen resembles her noble ancestors. Ironically, the ancestors they are talking about are the real queen's ancestors. In the soldiers' eyes, the regalia bring about a physical transformation to match the inner transfiguration.

> **3 SOLDIER** How could we leave you alone and in danger? I fought under your father. You have his eyes.
> **2 SOLDIER** I was with him too. You have the very colour of his hair.
> **3 SOLDIER** It is Your Majesty's walk that is most like.
> **P QUEEN** Oh, then if you see [?] my father in me, and fought under him, it was as though he spoke to you.¹⁴

Yeats discovered that he needed a separate channel for philosophy as he was writing plays. Such a channel was provided—though this was probably not the playwright's intention—by the many drafts of the play itself. The discursive early versions of major speeches give the impression that Yeats enjoyed toying with the ideas as much as he enjoyed playing with Gordon Craig's scale model screens that were of such use to him as he worked on this play. The fact that he was toying with these ideas, even though he originally conceived the play as tragedy, may have led him to the discovery that the play would achieve completion only as farce, a form that would permit him to mock the ideas as he expressed their seriousness.

The play's fundamental action embodies the triumph of imagination, of the mask. An energetic representative of mask and imagination in the finished play is the poet, by this time called Septimus. In a speech in an early draft dropped from the final version because it is subsumed into the action, Septimus inveighs against realism and chastises the audiences who demand it.

> They cannot have art because they do not know that we must always love what we are not: the coward loves courage, the sluggish energy, the sad delight, the foolish wisdom. But they, they [are] all cattle, no all pigs, loving the straw they lie on better than the clouds of dawn. No, this is not for them, this is a drama for kings.[15]

Though discursive defenses of poetry are excised from the finished play, the Prime Minister in the final version speaks a memorable defense of the realistic drama. The playwright is ever alive to the irony that this figure, an energetic proponent of the mask in the realm of politics, remains the play's staunchest defender of realism in the theater.

> I will not be trifled with. I chose the play myself; I chose the tragical history of Noah's deluge because when Noah beats his wife to make her go in to the ark, everybody understands, everybody is pleased, everybody recognizes this mulish obstinacy of their own wives, sweethearts, sisters. And now, when it is of the greatest importance to the state that everybody should be pleased, the play cannot be given. The leading lady is lost, you say, and there is some unintelligible reason why nobody can take her place; but I know what you are all driving at—you object to the play I have chosen. You want some dull, poetical thing, full of long speeches. I will have that play and no other.[16]

Yeats had been doing battle in pamphlets, speeches, and articles with people like the Prime Minister through all his years with the theater. Giving credible and vigorous life to an idea he opposed was difficult for him. No section of *The Player Queen* cost him as much trouble as the first half of the second scene which the Prime

Minister must dominate. The scene came right, as he wrote Brinsley McNamara, only when he decided to put the character in a "real rage" (L 657–58). This enabled the playwright to satirize the character and his position, and at the same time allowed the character to express the position with the utmost vigor of speech and action. Yeats's slightly distanced stance, his allowing the opposing ideas to engage in their mocking dance of conflict, enabled him to transform a potentially discursive speech into a sequence of dramatic and theatrical gusto.

Decima embodies the leading idea in the play's final version. Alive to imagination and myth, she assumes the desired mask. The actress is in the act of plunging a pair of scissors into her heart. Her action is perfectly serious; her weapon may draw a laugh. Since these scissors had been used to cut the costume she refused to wear, they are an ironically appropriate means of destruction for this mask-seeking woman. The real queen, fearful of her own martyrdom at the hands of the raging mob, rushes in and stops Decima. Seeing the Queen's regalia that she herself has always yearned for, Decima proposes a means of escape for both of them.

> **DECIMA**   If they could mistake me for you, you would escape.
> **QUEEN**   I could not let another die instead of me. That would be very wrong.
> **DECIMA**   O Your Majesty, I shall die whenever you do, and if only I could wear that gold brocade and those gold slippers for one moment, it would not be so hard to die.
> **QUEEN**   They say that those who die to save a rightful sovereign show great virtue.
> **DECIMA**   Quick, the dress!
>
> (CPL 270–71)

In a sequence of dramatic action from which discursive speech has been winnowed, the playwright depicts two persons, each seeking and finding her proper mask. As the Queen strips off her regalia, she reveals her nun-like habit under it and announces her intention to enter a convent. As Decima simultaneously assumes the queenly robes, the audience can observe her assuming the gesture and pose, the walk of a queen.

The normally loquacious Prime Minister, seeing that the woman on the throne is indeed a real queen, is struck dumb and compliant.

DECIMA Your emotion is too great for words. Do not try to speak.
PRIME MINISTER This . . . this . . .
DECIMA (standing up) I am Queen. I know what it is to be queen.
(CPL 272)

The journey from the discursive early drafts to these concise and effective scenes can serve as a model for the means by which thought in drama must be absorbed into the action. Several hundred draft lines of philosophic debate about mask and face, self and antiself, are distilled in a brief scene between Decima and Nona. Here, Yeats makes ironic use of a lyric he had written as he was beginning to explore the ideas of the mask, and had published in the *Green Helmet* volume, nine years before *The Player Queen* was first performed.

NONA You think that you have his every thought because you are a devil.
DECIMA Because I am a devil, I have his every thought. You know how his own song runs. The man speaks first. (singing)
"Put off that mask of burning gold
With emerald eyes." And then the woman answers:
"Oh no, my dear, you make so bold
To find if hearts be wild and wise
And yet not cold."
NONA His every thought! That is a lie! He forgets all about you the moment you are out of his sight.
(CPL 261–62)

Decima's speech with its embedded lyric apotheosizes the mask, but Nona, seeking no mask, has the lyric's author in her bed. In this brief masterful sequence, the playwright demonstrates the idea's virtues and limitations. Such a thoroughgoing dramatic probing could not have been carried out in discursive prose, in Yeats's earlier philosophic plays, or in the early drafts of this play.

The Player Queen was first performed in May 1919. In October 1917, Yeats's wife began the automatic writing from which he derived the ideas explored in two versions of *A Vision*, as well as in several other essays, poems, and plays. Though these ideas are not so thoroughly explored in drafts of *The Player Queen* as is the idea of the mask, they are thoroughly absorbed and mocked in that play's final version.

Nearly as important to the finished play as the idea of the mask is the idea, becoming central to Yeats's thought in the early twenties, that the current age will end, and that the new age will be heralded by a mythical, violent, bestial copulation (VB 263). The unlikely wearer of the mask of John the Baptist's counterpart as prophet for the new dispensation is Septimus, the beleaguered poet-playwright. Perpetually drunk, a braggart soldier of *belles lettres*, Septimus takes his prophet's role with deep seriousness. As with much comedy, the character's gravity is a source of the audience's laughter. This figure allows the playwright, as Seanchan and the Wise Man did not, to play with serious ideas without diminishing the spectators' sense of their seriousness.

One of the current dispensation's most powerful myths is that of the Good Samaritan, so when this myth loses its power, as it does in the opening moments of the play, the audience may be inclined to agree half-seriously with Septimus's conclusions.

> Robbed, so to speak; naked, so to speak; bleeding, so to speak; and they pass by on the other side of the street. (CPL 250)

Inherent in the action and language of one of Septimus's subsequent scenes is the idea that the world is about to change utterly, that a new dispensation is at hand. A revolutionary mob is coming to storm the palace. Convinced that their queen is a witch committing unnatural acts with a unicorn, their intention is to strangle her. Yeats's draft notes suggest that he was concerned about making the mob sufficiently dangerous. As in much great comedy, the line between farce and violence is all but erased. Darting in just ahead of the mob is Septimus, still drunk, blood on his face, speaking in prophetic fury.

> Gather about me, for I announce the end of the Christian era! The coming of a new dispensation, that of a new Adam, that of the unicorn! But alas, he is chaste, he hesitates, he hesitates! (CPL 265)

Septimus is playing with the notion that every new age needs its beast god, dove, swan, or sphinx, whose sexual act will bring the new order to birth. The audience can laugh at Septimus's frustration that the chaste unicorn rejects the assigned role.

One technique the playwright uses to advance the play's ideas is dramatic juxtaposition: That is, he presents the audience with several actions whose marked similarity encourages the spectators to explore the implied comparison. One sequence may serve as a deliberate metaphor for another, and an idea, at once mocked and seriously advanced, is inherent in the coupled metaphors. Septimus evokes a copulating unicorn as a herald for a new age. Meanwhile Decima flirts with the idea of copulating with all her fellow performers who, in preparation for the Noah play, are disguised as beasts. At her command, they perform an erotic dance which, like Septimus's evocation of the unicorn, heralds the new dispensation that Decima will bring to birth.

The old beggar, forever clamoring for straw, reinforces the notion of a new dispensation. Braying like a donkey to herald every change of power, the beggar calls to mind the donkey that carried Christ into Jerusalem (CPL 255). Here then is another beast intimately involved in the annunciation of a new era. The spectacle of a farcical old beggar that harbors an awesome unseen power becomes a perfect theatrical image of the play's seriocomic action.

Without pushing either idea too hard, and without choking either idea in the abstract language of doctrine, Yeats produces a stage work that plays with two of his central and most difficult ideas: the finding of the antithetical self and the coming to birth of an antithetical dispensation. These ideas join in a complex sequence that is one of the play's comic climaxes. With the mob in all its political and metaphysical turmoil about to storm the palace, the theater company in all its domestic and amorous turmoil rushes to escape. But the theatrical images and emblems, the very masks to which these men and women must be united, are left behind. On fire to save them, Nona piles them upon Septimus's back. Septimus, a student of metaphysical irony, immediately perceives the emblematic significance of what she is doing.

> It is necessary that we who are the last artists (all the rest have gone over to the mob) shall save the images and implements of our art . . . Tie all upon my back, and I will tell you the great secret that came to me at the second mouthful of the bottle. Man is nothing till he is united to an image. Now the unicorn is both an image and a beast. That is why he alone can be the new Adam. (CPL 267)

After the 1919 performances, Yeats tinkered with his play one more time, making a new ending. In the original performance the play had ended with Decima eating her lobster on her new throne and hurling the claw at her new husband with the memorable curtain line: "Crack the claw." In the new ending Yeats carries even further the play's dramatic exploration of its driving ideas. Decima calls the players before her, banishes them—they, after all, know too much about her former identity—and commands them to give her a parting dance. This dance, celebrating the coming of the new dispensation, parallels the erotic dance that had heralded that dispensation. Decima, now queen indeed, continues to seek a new antithetical self. She dons a mask from the very play of Noah that she had refused to perform in while she was still an actress. Having united with the image of Queen, she is now seeking to unite with her new opposite, the performer. Her newly written final speech suggests that she has grown to suit her new role, and that she is at the same time uncertain about it.

> You are banished, and must not return upon pain of death. And yet not one of you shall be poorer because banished. That I promise. But you have lost one thing that I will not restore. A woman player has left you. Do not mourn her. She was a bad, headstrong, cruel woman and seeks destruction somewhere and with some man she knows nothing of. Such a woman, they tell me, that this mask would well become—this foolish, smiling face. Come, dance! (CPL 273)

After almost a dozen years of work and with myriad rejected drafts behind him, Yeats had reached in this philosophical farce an apotheosis of the play of ideas revealed through exuberant action. It achieved the playwright's highest ideal for the sort of play that, beginning in philosophy, ends in life, biography, drama. Completely alive at last, it would seem to the hasty reader a mere story. One would think that, having made so successful a marriage between thought and drama, the playwright need no longer quarrel with himself and others about thought, so necessary to the life of the drama, and that life's enemy. Yet the dramatist did continue this quarrel throughout his writing life. In "On the Boiler," his late compendium of fluid ideas and frozen opinions, he returns once again to worry the problem of thought and action.

> But thought is not more important than action; masterpieces, whether of the stage or study, excel in their action, their visibility. . . . We are

not coherent to ourselves through thought but because our visible image changes slowly. (EXP 446)

The Resurrection first performed 1934

In *The Resurrection*, begun in 1925, published in *The Adelphi* in 1927, reworked and published again in 1932, and finally performed at the Abbey in 1934, Yeats attempted to make drama out of philosophic debate. He knew many of the ideas on which this play was based would be familiar to readers and audiences of *The Player Queen*, as well as to readers of *A Vision*, first published nine years earlier. Like *The Player Queen*, *The Resurrection* is also concerned with the shocking beginning of a new era: the Christian era whose violent end Septimus had prophesied in *The Player Queen*, is born violently here. The play is also concerned with eternal recurrence, an idea memorably set forth in the play's opening lyric:

> Another Troy must rise and set
> Another lineage feed the crow,
> Another Argo's painted prow
> Drive to a flashier bauble yet.
>
> (CPL 364)

Most difficult of all for purposes of dramatization, the play sets forth a debate in discursive prose about the nature of deity. The central situation could not be more compelling. On the Sunday morning after the Crucifixion, the remaining eleven disciples await an event whose nature they do not know, and every spectator does know. Outside the room where they wait, the frenzied worshipers of Dionysus are celebrating the god's death and expected ritual resurrection. As in *The Player Queen*, the playwright uses dramatic juxtaposition, inviting the audience to consider the connections of Dionysus to Christ and to meditate upon the death of gods.

But this is the offstage action. Spectators at this play must give most of their attention to what Yeats describes in a letter as "young men talking" (L 780). The central event is the newly risen Christ walking slowly and silently through the room, but there is a great deal of talk preceding that final entrance. The playwright adopts strategies to insure dramatic tension, but observers differ as to his success. Joseph Holloway, longtime Abbey playgoer and diarist, and not usually a fan of Yeats, notes: "As the characters have only to stand around and talk, there is nothing to produce about the piece."[17] Even Liam Miller, almost always generous in his appreciation of Yeats's plays, finds this one dramatically wanting. For him, the play "does not succeed in getting its meaning across in theatrical idiom, and it depends too much on expository dialogue with a lack of action to retain the interest of even the private audience of devotees to which it is addressed."[18]

In the play's final version, the discursive dialogue is given dramatic tension, but it remains discursive dialogue. The Greek and the Hebrew expound their opinions about the nature of deity as if they were in a classroom:

> **GREEK**   No, no! I'm laughing because they thought they were nailing the hands of a living man upon the cross: and all the time, there was nothing there but a phantom.
> **HEBREW**   I saw him buried.
> **GREEK**   We Greeks understand these things. No god has ever been buried. No god has ever suffered. Christ only seemed to be born, only seemed to eat, seemed to sleep, seemed to walk, seemed to die. I did not mean to tell you until I had proof.
> ....
> **HEBREW**   He was nothing more than a man: the best man who ever lived. Nobody before him had so pitied human misery. He preached the coming of the Messiah because he thought the Messiah would take it all upon himself. Then some day when he was very tired after a long journey perhaps, he thought that he himself was the Messiah. He thought it because of all destinies it seemed the most terrible.
> **GREEK**   How could a man think himself the Messiah?
> **HEBREW**   It was always foretold that he would be born of a woman.
> **GREEK**   To say that a god can be born of a woman, carried in her womb, fed upon her breast, washed as children are washed, it is a most terrible blasphemy.
>
> (CPL 366–67)

The audience is to imagine that the disciples are in an inner room, out of view of the spectators but visible to the young men on the stage. The window looking out on to the street where the worshippers of Dionysus are gathering is imagined to be behind the spectators. The young men, watching the increasing frenzy, can be staring directly into the audience, and the spectators can be implicated in the Dionysiac orgies. The dialogue, then, is always actuated by what the characters are seeing as they gaze either into the disciples' room or out the window. The performers must call upon all their resources of imagination to describe in sensuous detail what the characters are presumed to be seeing, and to infuse those descriptions with the requisite sympathy, horror, or astonishment. The passage quoted above, for example, is called forth when the Greek, looking out the window, sees the hill of Calvary with all its terrible associations, and bursts into uncontrollable laughter that energizes his speech. The Hebrew, by contrast, can be near or in tears as he gazes at the unseen, despairing disciples.

This anchoring of the young men's speech in their immediate, sensuous experience constitutes the most substantial improvement in the version Yeats published in 1932 and that was performed at the Abbey in 1934. Yeats had called the earlier version a "chaotic dialogue" (L 780), but he believed the new version had dramatic tension throughout. In the earlier version, for example, the characters embark on a discussion of the Dionysiac ritual that sounds, as Bradford points out, "rather like notes taken from *The Golden Bough*."[19] In the later version, the speeches on this ritual are prompted by what the characters see from their window. Staring at the audience, they watch in fascination and growing horror the transvestite dancers, the copulations, the rendings.

> It is the worshippers of Dionysus. They are under that window now. There is a group of women who carry upon their shoulders a bier with an image of the dead god upon it. No! They are not women! They are men dressed as women. I've seen something like it in Alexandria. They are all silent as if something were going to happen. My God, what a spectacle! (CPL 368)

After the famous opening song, the first three quarters of this short play consists of exposition, description, narration, intellection. Though the play's subject is interior change, this change is not revealed in dramatic action until the final few startling moments. Moreover, Yeats has burdened his play with other notable weaknesses. There is no great personality—no Deirdre, Cuchulain, or Cathleen ni Houlihan on this stage. These figures are quite ordinary young men, deliberately nameless, speaking in serviceable but hardly memorable prose. A point of the play is that they could be anyone.

Discursive talk as well as action is necessary to the play as Yeats conceives it. The young men's view of the world and that which lies beyond it is to be reconstituted. In order to apprehend the magnitude of the conversion, the audience must comprehend the young men's ideas and opinions through their talk. The setting forth of fixed philosophical positions is as necessary to the exposition in this play as is recapitulating the narrative of the Crucifixion and describing the Dionysiac ritual.

Only with the entrance of the Syrian, more than half way through the short play, do the characters' visible images begin to change. The Syrian is visibly changed by the news that he carries with him of the resurrection:

> I am like a drunken man. I can hardly stand upon my feet. Something incredible has happened. I have run all the way. (CPL 369)

In the midst of transfiguration there is still narrative and argument. The Syrian describes the Galilean women's famous encounter at the tomb, and all the young men speculate about how Peter and the others will react.

> If you told your story, they would no more believe it than I do. But Peter's misery would be increased. . . . Peter would remember that the women did not flinch, that not one amongst them denied her master, that the dream proved their love and faith. Then he would remember that he had lacked both, and imagine that John was looking at him. He would turn away and bury his head in his hands. (CPL 370)

Only in the final moments does thought fuse with onstage action. The Syrian begins to laugh, and his wild laughter embodies the forces his words evoke: "What if the irrational return? What if the circle begin again?" (CPL 371) The Greek, still clinging to the notion that Christ is a phantom lacking bones, sinews, and a beating heart, joins the laughter. Dionysiac frenzy sweeps the stage as the young men's laughter mixes with the musicians' crescendo of cries: "God has arisen" (CPL 371). The persons of the play at last embody the forces, human, phantom, and irrational that they have till now been only debating.

As the frenzy approaches its apotheosis, everyone on the stage becomes silent and still.

> **GREEK** Why are they all suddenly motionless? Why are all those unseeing eyes turned upon this house? Is there anything strange about this house?
> **HEBREW** Somebody has come into the room.
> (CPL 372)

As the figure of Christ appears onstage, each of the three young men is convinced that his opinion will be confirmed. Each is to be shocked into a larger and more comprehensive awareness.

> It has seemed to me of late that the sense of spiritual reality comes whether to the individual or to crowds from some violent shock, and that idea has the support of tradition. (VPL 935)

But this force too has been fed by "Man's own resinous heart." All the play's competing ideas fuse in the final moments of surpassing drama. The figure of Christ represents a new trinity: god as man, phantom, and irrational force. In so doing, he embodies a truth more complex and profound than any of the ideas articulated in the play's discursive speeches. This fusing of passion, thought, and image in a moment of dramatic discovery is a source of the unexampled dramatic power of the last few moments in *The Resurrection*. But in order to achieve that dramatic power, Yeats has had to articulate a fair amount of philosophy. In going against Goethe's maxim, of which he was so fond, he did not keep philosophy out of the play.

The Death of Cuchulain completed 1939

For the last decade of his life, Yeats continued to grapple with philosophy, passion's life and yet its enemy. However, he did not write another play that required discursive exposition. His five last plays, among his best, fuse action, image, and symbol, all informed by deep thought. But the thought is not, as in *The Resurrection*, explicitly articulated in dialogue. A late letter discussing the writing of Yeats's last play strikes a note of triumph: "I am writing a play on the death of Cuchulain, an episode or two from the old epic. My private philosophy is there, but there must be no sign of it. All must be like an old fairy tale. It guides me to certain conclusions, and gives me precision, but I do not write it. To me, all things are made of the conflict of two states of consciousness—beings or persons which die each others' life, live each others' death" (L 917).

As good as his word, Yeats does not write his philosophy, because, "Where there are no words, there is less to spoil" (CPL 439). Together with a prologue, a dance, and a song, the play consists of a series of brief, gnomic encounters that embody the conflict of two states of consciousness. But these states are not, as they are in *The Resurrection*, set out in plain prose. The only plain prose occurs in the prologue in which the old man, a Yeats surrogate who is at least part self-parody, states some of the playwright's best-known and most controversial opinions about theaters and audiences:

> If there are more than a hundred, I won't be able to escape people who are educating themselves out of the book societies and the like. Scholiasts all, pickpockets and opinionated bitches! Why pickpockets? I will explain that! I will make it all quite clear! (Drum and pipe behind the scene. Then silence.) (CPL 438)

In the spirit of *The Player Queen*, the playwright mocks his idea. He is never himself more frozen in opinion than when he is inveighing against opinion. The flourish of drum and pipe cutting off the abstract talk may be the last skirmish in Yeats's life-long war over the uses of philosophy in the theater.

There are no further discursive speeches in this brief play. "I make the truth!" is Cuchulain's defining statement. His actions and brief passionate speeches suggest that he views himself as an unchanging, perhaps grotesque relic of an irrecoverable past.

> You thought that if you changed, I'd kill you for it
> When everything sublunary must change.
> And if I have not changed, that goes to prove
> That I am monstrous.
>
> (CPL 441)

In the first of his encounters, he faces in Eithne and the Morigu the embodiments of love and war, the two forces that have governed his life. Without explaining his choice, he chooses to fight, knowing that he has been betrayed and that he will die in the coming battle.

In an enactment of the ideas set forth in "Per Amica Silentia Lunae" the wounded hero meets his blind opposite. As the blind man exults in the twelve pennies he will get for Cuchulain's head, Cuchulain contemplates his soul's journey.

> **CUCHULAIN** I say it is about to sing.
> **BLIND MAN** Ah! Ah!
>
> (CPL 444)

This scene is a dramatic enactment of the great dialogue of self and soul that is an informing theme of Yeats's lyric and dramatic work. The blind man's exhalation of pleasure mingles with the bird notes of Cuchulain's departing soul, as each dies the other's life, lives the other's death. A late Yeats letter may set forth, as Philip Marcus persuasively argues, a philosophical foundation for the play.[20] "The sensuous image is changed from time to time at predestined moments called initiationary moments. . . . When all the sensuous images are dissolved, we meet true death" (L 916–17).

The dissolution of sensuous images from Cuchulain's past may have been at the philosophical foundation of the play, just as a moral question had been at the philosophical foundation of *The Countess Cathleen*. But this thought is absorbed, as Yeats argues it should be in drama, into mere story. In his final play, Yeats the playwright adheres to a principle famously set forth in his last surviving letter. In a series of dramatic encounters, the persons on his stage embody a truth that cannot be known. His philosophy is there, but he does not write it. His last play illustrates a conclusion in his last essay: thought is not more important than action. But thought in this play, as in his best plays and his worst, is at the foundation of action. In his best plays, thought becomes a part of action, giving it weight and permanence.

5
The Playwright as Stage Machinist

The Spectacle has, indeed, an emotional attraction of its own, but, of all the parts, it is the least artistic, and connected least with the art of poetry. . . . Besides, the production of spectacular effects depends more on the art of the stage machinist than on that of the poet.
—*Poetics*

Words fail. There are times when even they fail.
—*Happy Days*

Looking back on the Abbey's early years, Augusta Gregory told the founders of the Chicago Little Theatre that the "Irish mistake was to confuse theatric with literary values . . . poetry must serve the theater before it can again rule there."[1] Yeats was never content that poetry should merely serve, and he never granted that his insistence on the primacy of the word was a mistake. Nonetheless, he knew that words could not be self-sufficient in the theater. He spent his working life groping his way toward theatrical practices his fellow Irish dramatists grasped from the beginning. Synge's Maurya rakes her turf fire, diminishing the heat that sustains the bread of life. Beckett's Estragon puffs and groans, trying vainly to take off his boot, and the effort prompts him to conclude: "Nothing to be done." Acknowledged masters of words, these playwrights made joyous use of all the theater's resources. During his first years with the theater, Yeats took little joy in what he believed to be "irrelevant distractions."[2] His dislike of the wearying business of preparing plays for production rings down the century: "My curse on plays / That have to be set up in fifty ways" (CP 104). Yet he reluctantly came to acknowledge that he must manage the physical resources of his stage: gesture, mask, scenic effect, color, light and shadow, as carefully as he managed and selected the details of plot, character, and dialogue.

5 / THE PLAYWRIGHT AS STAGE MACHINIST

During the early Abbey years, the budding playwright achieved his most striking and successful use of theatrical resources not in a play but in his staging of the theater's response to the pious nationalists who led the 1907 attacks on *The Playboy of the Western World*. Nine days after the audience famously broke up in disorder at the word "shift," Yeats defied the wishes of his fellow directors by producing a public debate on the Abbey stage in the presence of a hostile audience. The event proved a memorable instance of political theater. Its most striking images may have brought home to the apprentice dramatist how powerful the theater's forces could be, if properly deployed.

There were moments of comedy whose grotesquerie exceeded Synge's play: ladies left the theater in response to a medical student and friend of Joyce's frank description of rural frustration in marriage. A chief actor in the event, Yeats taught himself a memorable lesson about the effective fusion of comedy with rage. Costumed for the occasion "in regulation pince-nez and artistic bow-tie" he got his angry audience to laugh when he declared himself to have been "President of the Wolfe Tone Commemoration Committee of Great Britain." He then capped the laugh line in precise theatrical fashion with the ringing, if not wholly accurate, declaration: "The author of *Cathleen ni Houlihan* addresses you!"[3] The evening's most memorably theatrical image, a fitting response to a play about patricide, was that of Yeats's father:

> Before him a raging crowd:
> "This land of saints," and then as the applause died out,
> "Of plaster saints"; his beautiful mischievous head thrown back. (CP 349)

From the young Cuchulain declaring "I'll pay the debt that is owing" to the old Cuchulain declaring "I make the truth," the dramatist would ring many changes on this superbly staged image of a striking and lonely personality besting a knot of adversaries.

As with every theatrical event, the success of the Abbey's chief salvo in the fight over *The Playboy* depended on the joint labor of collaborating artists. Yeats's plays, many of them composed in collaboration, also required the participation of actors, dancers, sculptors, painters, and mask-makers who could understand and serve his unusual dramatic vision. His relationships with fellow artists were always paradoxical and troubled; some of his worst quarrels with Synge and

Gregory were occasioned by his ceaseless quest to find performers capable of verse tragedy. "For if I am to be any use ever in Ireland, I must get good performances."[4] Yet during his most active years of Abbey management, Yeats rarely achieved ideal performances of his plays. Lady Gregory, noting the contrast between performances of Yeats's plays and Synge's, wrote "It did make me a little sad as I watched *Playboy* to think how easily that sort of work comes to our players, and how long it will be before your plays can go as well all round."[5]

Yeats was lobbying hard for the Abbey's engagement of Florence Darragh for *Deirdre*, and his letters about her set forth his sense of how much a collaborator he felt he needed improved his own playwriting: "I thought at moments of her *Salome* and ventured and discovered subtleties of emotion I have never attempted before."[6] More than most modern writers, Yeats subscribed to the myth of solitariness. Yet as this letter suggests, he needed to fuse his vision and talent with those of other theater artists. He made his greatest advances as a playwright when he entered into creative partnerships with Augusta Gregory, Gordon Craig, Edmund Dulac, Michio Itow, and Ninette de Valois.

But the playwright and theater manager always imposed a strong and often domineering will upon his collaborators. Though experience made him less rigid, he always hated over-emphatic speech and distracting motion on the stage. At one point, he half-seriously contemplated putting the performers in barrels and moving them about himself with a pole (EXP 86). He deemed economy and power of gesture as important a stage resource as economy and power of language.

For him, theatrical power derived from precision and simplicity—from the suggestive rather than the mimetic. As early as 1897, he was calling for a forest pattern rather than a forest painting, and he always insisted on a color scheme as simple as possible. "Two predominant colours in remote, fanciful plays—one colour predominant in actors, one in backcloth."[7] With scant theater experience and with what many observers believed to be dubious theatrical talent, Yeats had developed strong ideas about theatrical presentation: "A production that disturbs and obstructs the actor should be abandoned at once" (MEM 277).

The skeptical Holloway offers a portrait of Yeats at work in the theater.

a more irritating play producer never directed a rehearsal. He's ever flitting about and interrupting the players in the middle of their speeches, showing them by illustration how he wishes it done, droningly reading this passage and that in monotonous preachy sing-song, or climbing up the ladder on the stage and pacing the boards as he would have the players do. Ever and always he was on the fidgets, and made each and all of the players inwardly pray backwards. Frank Fay, I thought, would explode with suppressed rage at his frequent interruptions during the final speeches he had to utter.[8]

Holloway's description points to one of the most troubling paradoxes of the modern theater. Theatre is a collaborative art; yet every theater artist requires absolute control over materials and resources, and especially over the interpretation and execution of collaborating artists. Yeats was not alone in his rage for control. Every important theater artist of modern and most probably of ancient times has been an autocrat. Beckett biographer James Knowlson describes the playwright trying to induce actress Brenda Bruce, as Winnie in *Happy Days*, to speak to a metronomically strict rhythm, "At one stage he even brought a metronome into the theater and set it down on the floor, saying, 'This is the rhythm I want.' To the actress's astonishment, he then left it ticking relentlessly away."[9]

Every aspect of the theater Yeats was laboring to invent can be illustrated by the playwright's often exhilarated, occasionally uneasy relations with the pioneering scenographer Gordon Craig. Working with director Nugent Monck in one of his most fruitful periods of theatrical collaboration, Yeats made extensive use of Craig's screens in the 1911–12 Abbey revivals of *The Countess Cathleen*, *The Land of Heart's Desire*, and *The Hourglass*. Craig's novel approach to the use of stage space—flexible, fluid, suggestive—opened a new world of theatrical possibility to the playwright who had raged so long against "a prison-house of paint" (VPL 1289).

But Yeats and Craig disagreed absolutely as to the senses to which the theater must make its principal appeal. Yeats's primary appeal was to the ear. By contrast, Craig distrusted words: "Poets would make the theater for a select company of dilletanti. They would put difficult psychological thoughts before the public, expressed in difficult words, and would make for this public something which was impossible for them to understand and unnecessary for them to know; whereas the theater *must show them sights*, show them life, show them beauty and not speak in difficult sentences."[10] When Craig describes what the modern poet/playwright has forgotten, and what the ancient dramatist/performer had always known, implied contrast to and criticism of Yeats is obvious. Craig's ideal ancient

> knew that when he and his fellows appeared in front of them, the audience would be more eager to see what he would do than to hear what he might say. He knew that the eye is more swiftly and powerfully appealed to than any other sense, that it is without question the keenest sense of the body of man. The first thing which he encountered on appearing before them was many pairs of eyes, eager and hungry. Even the men and women sitting so far from him that they would not always be able to hear what he might say seemed quite close to him by reason of the piercing keenness of their questioning eyes.[11]

It is hard to overestimate Yeats's debt to Craig, yet early in their association the playwright recognized their differences. Responding to a production of Ibsen's *Vikings of Helgaland*, Yeats wrote Gregory in April, 1903, "Craig's scenery is amazing but rather distracts one's thoughts from the words" (L 398). Though Yeats and Craig would reinforce each other in exercising control over any other theater artists with whom they might work, the need of each for absolute control and their mutual recognition of their fundamental differences precluded their prolonged collaboration. Yeats's plays for dancers, depending as they did on mask and controlled movement, might never have come into being but for Craig, but it was inconceivable that Yeats work with Craig on their production.

Years before Yeats and Pound began reading Fenollosa's accounts of the Noh, Craig was encouraging the playwright to use masks in revivals of *The Hourglass* and *On Baile's Strand*. In Craig's writings about the mask, he emphasized qualities that became important to Yeats. The mask is "always repeating unerringly the poetic fancy—repeating on Monday in 1912 exactly what it said on Saturday in 1909, and what it will say on Wednesday in 1999. Durability was the dominant idea in Egyptian art. The theater must learn that lesson. . . . Let us again cover [the actor's] face with a mask in order that his expression, the visualized expression of the poetic spirit, shall be everlasting."[12]

Craig's and Yeats's joint enthusiasm for the mask derived in part from the measure of control its use afforded over increasingly fractious productions. They heartily agreed upon covering the actor's

5 / THE PLAYWRIGHT AS STAGE MACHINIST

face with a mask and controlling the actor's movements and gestures as one might control those of a marionette. Putting into practice one of Craig's most complex and controversial theories, Yeats directed that the Old Man's movements in *At the Hawk's Well,* "like those of the other persons of the play, suggest a marionette" (CPL 138). Craig had invented the idea of the "*Uebermarionette*," "the actor plus fire minus egotism—the fire of the gods and demons without the smoke and steam of mortality."[13]

Yeats had as little tolerance as Craig for any performer's uncontrolled interpretation. He was bent on creating an art that was self-sufficient, precise, controlled. He hated unnecessary movement, and he grew certain that the choreographed movements of the entire body, which could evolve into dance, would suggest more to his audience's imagination than the actor's too rapidly changing face. The mask would enable the playwright to prevent the actor's personality from interfering with the expression, in precisely chosen words and gestures, of the personality of Cuchulain.

In a famous passage first published in Craig's *The Mask* Yeats had written: "The persons upon the stage, let us say, greaten till they are humanity itself" (E and I 245). This greatening of the tragic figure was achieved through a concomitant lessening of the spontaneous, uncontrolled humanity of the performer representing him. The playwright was infuriated during the final days of rehearsal for *At The Hawk's Well* by Henry Ainlee who, as Cuchulain, "waves his arms like a drowning kitten. . . . I am going this afternoon to Dulac to go on working out gestures for Ainlee. They are then to be all drawn by Dulac" (L 609).

T. S. Eliot, also seeking to master the intractable elements and resources of the theater, had similar expectations. He wrote that no "modern actor, with his interpretive gifts, would allow the poetry to reach the audience. . . . For poetry is something which the actor cannot improve or interpret; . . . in consequence, the ideal actor for a poetic drama is the actor with no personal vanity."[14]

Yeats required as well a high degree of technical skill and a knowledge and love of verse. Actors needed the ability to fit their voices into the verse rhythms and cadences, and fit their bodies into the gestures and movements. Given Yeats's demands and his rage for control, it is a tribute to the strength of his vision and to his ability as a theatrical manager that he persuaded so many able performers and designers to submit to his control and help him shape his unusual and unpopular form of theater. Though he wore himself out with the Abbey, and though he was often bitterly disappointed, many of his plays called forth memorable performances and designs.

The Green Helmet first performed 1910

The Green Helmet, the play that marked the end of its author's Abbey apprenticeship, was inspired by the years of theatrical quarrels and frustrations. At the same time, there is a liberating exuberance about the play that suggests the dramatist's hardwon theatrical mastery. Cuchulain, at the height of his powers, learns that two of his friends have lost a head-chopping contest to a mysterious Red Man wearing a green helmet who has come up out of the sea. When the Red Man's head was cut off, he coolly picked it up, put it under his arm, and went his way with a promise to return a year later for their heads. In a generous gesture of self-sacrifice, Cuchulain undertakes to pay the Red Man's debt.

"Two colours and a third for accent" became the guiding principle of design. This play's two colors were the green of the helmet, the sea, and the cloaks of the combatants, contrasted with the orange-red of the setting, matched by the red of the Red Man. The third color was the black of the room's furnishings and the surrounding rocks. In the play's original prose version, the contested helmet had been golden. In the revision, the helmet changed color so as to match the garments of the contending warriors and to show up better against the orange background. At the play's climax, the green-clad Cuchulain confronts the Red Man, with the green helmet between them. The strife between orange-red and green can hardly have been lost on the 1910 Dublin audience.

The violent and startling visual images lend a disturbing aspect to the boisterous, exuberant action. The stage image enriches the words which can move from bouncy bravado to a serious, near-tragic lyricism. In performance, the play is anarchic modernist comedy that at times adumbrates Brecht or Dario Fo. As the stage grows crowded—Yeats had never before and would never again put so many people on the stage—and as the action grows increasingly violent, there are opportunities aplenty for concerted, precisely choreographed movement. Yeats in a 1909 letter (L 524), had observed that he was discovering a talent as a comic stage manager. Writing for this emerging talent, Yeats composed in *The Green Helmet* an invitation and challenge to all comic stage directors. Cuchulain's first entrance, taking advantage of a dip in the floor to shove the other kings out of his way, requires farcical stylization. So does the sequence in which Conall and Laegaire interrupt each other in spilling out their shame and fear that the Red Man will come to claim his debt from them.

> **CONALL**   And thinking that if we told it we should be a laughing-stock
> Swore we should keep it secret.
> **LAEGAIRE**   But twelve months upon the clock—
> **CONALL**   A twelvemonth from the first time—
> **LAEGAIRE**   And the jug full up to the brim:
> For we had been put from our drinking by the very thought of him—
> (CPL 151)

This stychomythic passage with its pronounced beat presents a comic duo that anticipates the Marx brothers or Gogo and Didi.

The action resolves itself into three successive quarrels, each more raucous than the last. Yeats's usually decorous stage is filled with the noise of blaring horns, clashing weapons and pots, bawling voices, and the final near-demolition of the scenery. Mirroring the stylized dialogue, the action moves toward tragicomic apocalypse.

The dramatist shows himself throughout to be a master of contrasting moods. In the midst of the most violent and shrill of the three quarrels, that among the wives, the percussive sound made by the beating down of sections of wall ceases for a moment as Emer sings a love song. Her lyric dimeters make for as strong a contrast with the thuds and cries as the orange-red makes with the green. For this moment, the play balances heroism with farce, comprehending both aspects of its descriptive subtitle.

The play's climax is a surrealist explosion, and Yeats understandably expected to have difficulty staging it.[15] As the quarrel reaches its height of concerted movement and noise, a black hand—black is the play's third color—reaches into the room and douses the orange-red light of this beleaguered interior. For all its hilarious theatrics, the play here achieves a striking discord. The dark, broken house is an image of Yeats's Ireland, torn by internecine strife. Without words, the playwright distills for a moment on the stage all the bitterness and rage of the lyrics published in the volume that bears the play's name. He then allows the action to turn upward toward the final fantasy of reconciliation. After a few seconds of blackness, a new, sea-green light fills the stage, setting off the Red Man and his black hordes. Set against this new green light, the action comprehends and transcends farce. Using the undercutting language of comedy, "Quick to your work, old radish" (CPL 158), Cuchulain offers a genuine sacrifice. The play's final speech too, the famous praise of the heroic Cuchulain, has its note of sobriety and loss. "Till a day come that I know / When heart and mind shall darken, that the weak may end the strong" (CPL 159). This rollicking, noisy play emerges as a surprising triumph of its maker's theatrical art. It is a worthy companion to Synge's meditative tragedy of Deirdre, to which it served as curtain-raiser.

The Countess Cathleen first published 1892; first performed 1899

With its crowded stage and blaring noise, *The Green Helmet* remained outside the playwright's main line of development. In an early summation of his aesthetic, he had written that "all art is, indeed, a monotony in external things for the sake of an interior variety; a sacrifice of gross effects to subtle effects, an asceticism of the imagination" (E and I 18).

As Yeats revised *The Countess Cathleen*, he sacrificed some gross theatrical effects, and though he was finally not wholly satisfied with the play, he did manage to achieve a measure of subtlety in his uses of the theater. When he first composed the play in 1891–92, he had virtually no theater experience. In 1911, under Craig's influence and in a happy collaboration with Nugent Monck, he produced at the Abbey an important production of the play—the first since the 1899 performance that launched the Irish dramatic movement. A comparison of the 1892 version with the play in its final form—benefiting from the work with Craig and Monck—reveals the imposition of limits and the achievement, within those limits, of variety, power, and some measure of subtlety.

For the 1892 version the inexperienced playwright imagined a stage filled with table, chairs, and other domestic objects. In the play's opening moments, Shemus enters with a dead wolf on his shoulder. For the play's final version, Yeats swept his stage clear of window, pantry, pot, furniture, and shrine. The theatrical uses to which these objects were put in the early version were absorbed in the final version into language and ritual action.

In the first version, the playwright achieved his most startling theatrical effects through a manipulation of objects. The dead wolf, the quicken branch to which it is tied, and the Catholic shrine figure largely in the entrance of the demon merchants.

> (Shemus begins unfastening the feet of the wolf from a branch to which they had been tied.)
> **MARY**   That's quicken wood. . . . (He takes up the branch to throw it on the fire.)
> **MARY**   (taking it from him) Shemus! Shemus!
> What, would you burn the blessed quicken wood?
> A spell to ward off demons and ill fairies.
> You know not what the owls were that peered in,
> For evil wonders live in this old wood.
>
> (VPL 20)

The evil merchants Mary fears knock and enter. They command Shemus to burn the sacred quicken bough. Then they seat themselves on chairs upon each side of the fire with the table between them. They empty their bags on the table, covering it with gold pieces. The scene is thus dominated by symbolic props: the glittering gold and the burning sacred bough. The scene's most arresting moment comes about through the manipulation of another symbolic prop: the shrine falls from the wall as the demon merchants appear. The theatrically inexperienced Yeats might not, in 1892, have realized how difficult it is to control such an event on the stage.

In future versions, his important effects depended less upon objects than upon actors. The version featuring the dead wolf and the falling shrine was never performed. For the final version, performed many times, Yeats introduced into the opening scene an entrance for Cathleen, Aleel, and Oona. In the original version, the eponymous heroine does not appear until the second scene, and the poet Kevin, Aleel's counterpart in the early version, does not appear until Scene IV. It can be argued that the early appearance of Cathleen and her entourage is problematic: Frazier wonders drily how the countess can be lost in her own wood.[16] Yet Cathleen's appearance in Shemus's cottage makes possible a number of subtle and powerful theatrical juxtapositions. Immediately preceding the entrance, Aleel's instrument is heard offstage. Shemus's hostile reaction is quick and strong. His lines: "Who's passing there / And mocking us with music?" (CPL 4) with Aleel playing under them, establish the antipathy between Aleel and the spirits of negation that will reach a dramatic climax in the final scene. The theatrical antipathy deepens as Aleel sings his defiant love lyric under Shemus's nose. This song provides the audience's first intimation—set forth in an effectively oblique theatrical manner—that the poet is in love with the countess. The singing and playing comprise an early example of the playwright's rich and complex uses of music and song throughout his plays. Cathleen's contrast in appearance, manner, and dress with Shemus and his family establishes, as the early version does not, a set of dynamic, mutual obligations between rich and poor.

> So you are starving, even in this wood
> Where I had thought I would find nothing changed;
> But that's a dream, for the old worm of the world
> Can eat its way into what place it pleases. (She gives money.)
>
> (CPL 5)

Her small purse makes possible a contrasting image of evil plenitude when the merchants produce their cascades of gold. More important, her words and action suggest that the countess, for all her vague benevolence is, at the very least, culpably ignorant of matters on her estate. Her initial response to the spectacle of starvation is almost aesthetic, giving some credence to Shemus's bitter words: "What is the trouble of the poor to her? / Nothing at all, or a harsh radishy sauce / For the day's meat" (CPL 4). Her resolve in the second scene to combat the famine, first with physical and then with spiritual means, gathers enormous theatrical power from its implicit contrast with her first reaction in Shemus's cottage.

Aleel's confrontation with Shemus climaxes in a moment of lyric drama that the playwright himself long remembered. Aleel's lines, spoken in an incantatory manner and on only a few notes, would infuse with suggestive power the subsequent entrance of the demon merchants. Yeats recalled the performance in *Dramatis Personae*.

> Nothing satisfied me but Florence Farr's performance in the part of Aleel. Dublin talked of it for years, and after five-and-thirty years I

keep among my unforgettable memories the sense of coming disaster she put into the words: "But now, / Two grey horned owls hooted above our heads." (AU 279)

In the 1892 version, Mary and Teig call attention to the horned owls in conventionally Christian terms that lack Aleel's concision and force.

> **MARY** Think upon your soul.
> What made that noise?
> **TEIG** Two horned owls made it;
> They have been blinking on the window-sill
> Since father came.
>
> (VPL 18)

With a stringed instrument and lyric power, Aleel in Shemus's cottage prefigures the musicians in Yeats's dance plays. His resemblance in form and function to these musicians is further strengthened by a brief new scene the playwright made for the 1911 revival. Played in front of the curtain, the new scene permitted a massive scene change to take place without a break in the action. This scene, dominated by Aleel's song "Impetuous Heart Be Still," brings about the sort of contrast in mood and meter that becomes a mainstay of the dance plays.

The dance plays are anticipated as well by the manner of the demon merchants' entrance in the later version. The sequence begins with Shemus's formal act of conjuration, not dissimilar to the musicians' conjuration in Yeats's first dance play of the dry well and the stripped hazels.

> Whatever you are that walk the woods at night,
> So be it that you have not shouldered up
> Out of a grave, for I'll have nothing human,
> And have free hands—a friendly trick of speech—
> I welcome you; come sit beside the fire!
>
> (CPL 7)

The entrance immediately following Shemus's speech is prolonged and deliberately stylized. Played on the Abbey stage in 1911, this entrance may have given the playwright ideas about the theatrical power of ritualized, controlled movement. "Teig lifts one arm slowly and points toward the door and begins moving backward. Shemus turns. He also sees something and begins moving backward. Mary does the same. A man dressed as an Eastern merchant comes in, carrying a small carpet. He unrolls it and sits cross-legged at one end of it. Another man dressed in the same way follows and sits at the other end. This is done slowly and deliberately. When they are seated, they take money out of embroidered purses at their girdles and begin ranging it on the carpet." (CPL 8) It is a relatively small step from this play's merchants unrolling the carpet to the dance plays' musicians folding and unfolding the cloth.

But even in the play's revised version, there is an uneasy mixture of ritual with mimetic realism. Shemus strikes his wife before he conjures the demons. The realistic blow jars with the demons' stylized entrance. The later Yeats would devise theatrical forms of stylized violence—as in *The Cat and the Moon, The Herne's Egg,* or *The Death of Cuchulain.* In each of these plays, cymbal clashes represent blows, and the revenge act takes the form of a dance. But the later Yeats, theatrical mastery evolving, would not mix theatrical modes as does the Yeats of *The Countess Cathleen.*

Between the 1892 and 1911 versions of this play, the playwright moved decidedly away from an almost farcical realism and tentatively toward the austere, suggestive mode of the dance plays. In its earliest version, this is a cluttered play. The merchants break up the furniture and burn the food. Unwilling tevishes and other creatures troop onto the stage. The demon merchants, in farcical fashion, lose the souls they have gathered through holes torn in the bags they are using for collection. In revising for theatrical production the playwright, now faced with actual stage conditions and the necessity of economizing, eliminated most of these actions and objects. On a stage almost free of furniture, a good deal of dramatic power can derive from a single object. But none of the objects that appeared on the stage in the 1899, or even the 1911, production can be described as an anchoring symbol that embodies in palpable form the play's actions and ideas. Though the author of the lyrics that would comprise *The Wind Among the Reeds* and the essays on symbolism in painting and poetry had by 1899 mastered the uses of symbols in nondramatic verse, the author of *The Countess Cathleen,* still very much an apprentice dramatist, was groping toward assurance as a stage symbolist.

By the time of the first performance of *The Countess Cathleen,* the most accomplished stage symbolist of his age was Henrik Ibsen.

When We Dead Awaken, produced the same year as *The Countess Cathleen,* exercised enormous influence on the young James Joyce. But Yeats underestimated Ibsen—never fully acknowledging the Norwegian's ability to invest objects—a stove, a portrait, an unseen captive duck—with the power and resonance of anchoring symbols. The anchoring symbol is most effective when it is central to a scene marked by austerity and dramatic economy, fundamentally unlike the final scene of *The Countess Cathleen*'s first version. In this scene, the untried playwright is crowding onto the stage both the creatures of Irish fairy lore and the assembled angelic hosts that represent medieval Christianity. In this scene's most arresting moment, Oona finds the oratory steps covered with feathers and says, "Some hawk or kestrel, chased its prey to this; / These are owl's feathers" (VPL 160). More than anything else on the stage in this scene, these feathers give concrete reality and theatrical power to the sense of otherworldly evil the play seeks to create. They make clear, as no mere words can, that the merchants are simultaneous inhabitants of two worlds. These feathers constitute, as David R. Clark demonstrates, an anchoring symbol. Clark argues persuasively that in eliminating the feathers from the play's later versions, Yeats is swerving away from dramatic vision in the interests of theatrical construction.[17] But the early version's faulty theatrical construction diminishes the power of this most important symbol. The owl's feathers are all but lost on a stage teeming with activity and full of objects. In its first unstaged version, *The Countess Cathleen* lacks theatrical form to express its author's vision. In Yeats's later plays, as in his lyric poetry, form and vision fuse through myriad revision. Through *The Countess Cathleen* in its various versions, the apprentice playwright was learning how performers moving through a lighted space could communicate his evolving dramatic vision. Though the play never wholly satisfied its maker, his long labor on it helped him achieve the assured use and radical reshaping of the theater's resources and techniques that were to distinguish his post-1916 plays.

Nowhere is the playwright's dissatisfaction and uncertainty about this play more apparent than in his treatment of the ending. In the revised play published after the 1911 Abbey production, Yeats included an ending different from that which he and Monck had staged. "I have left the old end, however, in the version printed in the body of this book, because the change for dramatic purposes has been made for no better reason than that audiences—even at the Abbey Theatre—are almost ignorant of Irish mythology—or because a shallow stage made the elaborate vision of armed angels upon a mountainside impossible" (VPL 173). The ending as printed resembles the final moments of Strindberg's *Ghost Sonata* in that it fleetingly depicts a better world than ours.

> (The darkness is broken by a visionary light. The peasants seem to be kneeling upon the rocky slope of a mountain and vapour full of storm and ever-changing light is sweeping above them and behind them. Half in the light half in the shadow stand armed angels. Their armour is old and worn, and their drawn swords dim and dinted. They stand as if upon the air in formation of battle and look downward with stern faces. The peasants cast themselves on the ground.) (CPL 31)

In the ending as staged at the Abbey, the playwright makes a concession to his audience's supposed ignorance of Irish legend and its presumed knowledge of Bible and Apocrypha by having Aleel refer not to Balar and Barach the traitor, but instead to fat Asmodel and giddy Belial. More theatrically germane is the excision, owing to the Abbey's shallow stage, of the vision of armed angels. In the play as performed at the Abbey, this vision existed in Aleel's mind. Anticipating the musicians in the dance plays, the poet used lyric speech to conjure his vision to the mind's eyes of the spectators.

> Angels and devils clash in the middle air,
> And brazen swords clang upon brazen helms.
> Look, look, a spear has gone through Belial's eye!
> (VPL 176)

In the ending as staged, the spectators saw only the angel that Aleel seized and questioned. Clark argues that in cutting the vision of armed angels, the playwright is once again revising away from the play's informing vision. Yeats's own ambivalence is evident in his decision not to publish the ending as it had been staged. Yet characteristics of the Abbey ending anticipate his mature dramaturgy.

The lyric conjuring of a difficult vision was to become a staple of the dance plays. Aleel's battle with the angel on the Abbey stage resembled Cuchulain's confrontation with the Red Man in being an early embodiment of what was to become a fundamental principle of Yeats's dramatic method: the battle of human and nonhuman antagonists.[18] Aleel wrings from an otherworldly creature, a visible manifestation of his own inner vision, the declaration that Cathleen "is passing to the floor of peace." On a stage not covered by an army of angels, this battle can be astonishing in its theatrical power.

In a production directed by Derek Chapman staged at the Yeats Summer School in Sligo in 1997, I was one of two performers who, acting together, played the angel as a two-bodied creature. One body was sighted but voiceless, the other was able to speak but not to see. Our staging reinstated the names of the Irish demigods and traitors, but like the 1911 Abbey production, our production had no army of angels. Instead, Aleel forced the angel to speak by ripping the sighted, speechless half from the blind half that could speak. In a voice in which I tried to express the agony of being halved, I spoke the angel's lines. In our production, as in the 1911 Abbey production, Aleel had battled an inhuman antagonist and had received news from a world other than our own. Judging from our audience's reaction, Aleel's battle with the angel and its result made for a most effective piece of Yeatsian theater.

In the Abbey ending, the audience's attention is concentrated on those left behind, the mourning Aleel and Oona, whose grief is scarcely assuaged by the joy of Cathleen's apotheosis. In the published ending, not performed at the Abbey, the human spectacle is subsumed by an unearthly vision of eerie and complex power. Oona's final speech is juxtaposed with a vision of embattled angels whose number Cathleen seems to be joining. An energy other than the energy of human life dominates the published ending, and an otherworldly, haunted state is briefly achieved. The published ending, as Clark demonstrates, fits the play's vision of a victory beyond earthly limits; the staged ending conforms to the playwright's evolving vision of a battle where one antagonist does not wear a human face. As in the plays of his dramatic maturity, the playwright concentrates in the staged ending on that battle's effects on the human contestants. Aleel and Oona, dazed with grief, take their places with the unforgiving young man alone on a desolate mountain, with Emer watching her reclaimed husband in Eithne's arms, and with the wretched old man crying to an unseen God to appease the misery of the living.

Though he hated conventional realism, Yeats craved reality in the theater. With the merchants' stylized unfolding of the carpet, Aleel's songs, and the staging of the final battle between the poet and the angel, he affirmed and celebrated the reality of the theatrical: "I wish to have the stage itself real, though it must always suggest a dream. I would not disguise the real properties and the real light and shadow of the stage, and I would recognize the reality of the actor so much that I would put him against some plain unbroken surface that will display every movement. I would not allow any bad landscape painter to compete with him."[19]

The Abbey staging of *The Countess Cathleen*, together with its subsequent staging of *The Hourglass*, enriched the playwright's theatrical vocabulary. Yet for all their anticipation of Yeats's mature dramaturgy, both plays remain theatrical hybrids. The old-fashioned allegory of *The Hourglass* was only half sloughed off. In the revised *Countess Cathleen*, older and newer uses of theatrical resources are engaged in difficult conflict. One can detect such conflict in the revised final scene—both in its published and performed versions. Borrowing a gesture from *King Lear*, Oona ascertains that Cathleen has stopped breathing by holding a looking-glass over the Countess's lips. In a gesture that smacks of Victorian melodrama by way of *Richard II*, Aleel flings the mirror to the floor. "I shatter you in fragments, for the face / That brimmed you up with beauty is no more" (CPL 30). Samuel Beckett spoofs just such a gesture when Winnie in *Happy Days* shatters a mirror, knowing that "it will be in the bag again tomorrow without a scratch to help me through the day." Aleel's dramaturgically old-fashioned shattering of the mirror makes for an odd dissonance in a scene theatrically dominated by the peculiarly Yeatsian battle between poet and angel.

The King of the Great Clock Tower **first performed 1934**

By the time of his last plays, Yeats had developed a dramaturgy capable of giving theatrical concreteness to his otherworldly vision. In 1934, he achieved an unexpected triumph with *The King of the Great Clock Tower*. The play's silent queen forms a mysterious relation with a nameless stroller. Her husband has the stroller beheaded, and the silent queen dances in frenzy with the severed head.

The master of words fashioned silence into one of the play's most striking theatrical characteristics.

> Why sit you there

5 / THE PLAYWRIGHT AS STAGE MACHINIST

> Dumb as an image made of wood or metal
> A screen between the living and the dead?
> All persons here assembled—and because they think
> That silence unendurable, fix eyes
> Upon you. (There is a pause. The queen neither speaks nor moves.)
>
> (CPL 399)

The queen's silence is due at least in part to theatrical exigency. Yeats created the role for Ninette de Valois, the great nonspeaking dancer with whom he had worked in *Fighting the Waves*. Often in Yeats, theatrical exigency coincides with the play's metaphoric needs. As in the plays of Strindberg and Beckett, silence in this play is a source of strength, and the querulous king who tries to probe or break it exhibits weakness. Equally effective as the queen's silence is Yeats's theatrical use of the attendants' speech. These choric figures lend their voices to any personages the story needs. One attendant speaks for the Captain of the Guard. The other, in one of the play's most chilling moments, gives her voice to the hitherto silent queen.

Yeats's use of deliberately undisguised theatrical resources places him, as Flannery, Worth and others have demonstrated, in the modern European tradition that extends from Maeterlinck to Beckett and beyond. Like Beckett in the conclusion of *Happy Days*, Yeats combines silence, stillness, and song in his play's final tableau. Having completed her dance of sexual adoration to the severed head, the silent queen stands framed between the curtains while the attendant sings the last lines.

> Nobody knows what may befall,
> Said the wicked, crooked, hawthorn tree;
> I have stood so long by a gap in the wall
> Maybe I shall not die at all.
>
> (CPL 403)

In the person of the masked dancer, the queen perhaps defies, perhaps becomes, the song's enduring tree. The dancer's body, the attendant's voice, and the playwright's words create a compelling and mysterious theatrical image.

The queen's mystery is never penetrated, so it suffuses the play. But the playwright, veering between his need for a popular audience and his lifelong desire for a secret society of the arts (VPL 1009;

EXP 254), may have burdened the play with unnecessary obscurities, thus blurring and diminishing its essential mystery. The play's Abbey success, according to Holloway's account, derived largely from de Valois's dancing and from F. J. MacCormack's beautiful speaking voice. Yet even the performers remained baffled by the play to which they were giving stage life. Before it opened, MacCormack, who played the king, breathed a prayer to the playwright. "Well may the spirit of Mr. Yeats be with us tonight. And may it spread itself a bit and give a clue to the audience as to what it all is that we be talking about."[20]

Ninette de Valois described her work with Yeats as instinctual and noted that her choreography took shape from the music: "And for me, it was only a question of understanding what had inspired him and then letting the same feeling and approach inspire me. That was all there was to it. I don't claim to understand the play, but one had to feel something to achieve a quiet approach to them . . . I used movement that was highly stylized. The dances were very abstract. Masked, you couldn't be anything else."[21]

A Full Moon in March completed 1935

In his never-ceasing quest for simplicity, Yeats began rewriting *The King of the Great Clock Tower* very soon after its successful 1934 performance. In the new version, soon to take on a new identity and a new title, the antagonists are the poet—brutalized from stroller to swineherd—and the queen, self-proclaimed embodiment of virgin cruelty. The contrasting voices of the queen and the swineherd are echoed by the similarly contrasting voices—one a soprano, one a bass—of the two attendants. These attendants present and frame the action with music and lyrics, but they differ significantly from their counterparts in previous dance plays. In *At the Hawk's Well* and *The Dreaming of the Bones*, the musicians are the master-spirits, conjuring and controlling the action. The attendants in *A Full Moon in March* are not creatures from "some country of our dreams," conducting the yet unknowing audience into the deeps of the mind. Instead, like the audience, they are uncertain and unmasked explorers. The playwright scores their opening dialogue for contrasting voices: the high voice asks the questions, the low voice answers them, and the high voice suggests the eerie, thematic song. The attendants seem to discover from their own intuition—from that same place of vision to which the playwright himself seeks to appeal—what part they are to take in this enactment. Their journey from uncertainty to awe mirrors the journey of the audience.

With a masterly fusion of language and gesture, the attendants set forth the terms of the play's conflict as they initiate its action. The second attendant, with his bass voice, sings the opening song about the dung of swine, thereby establishing his affinity with the swineherd. The first attendant joins the singing on the final line: "Crown of gold or dung of swine." Singing together in their contrasting voices, the two attendants draw the inner curtain and discover the queen. Even before the queen speaks and moves, the attendants use these simple theatrical means to suggest that she is drawn to the levelling, transforming properties of love. The play's opposites are merged, both in the song and in the way of its singing at the precise moment that the queen is discovered. With its evocation of transformation and fusion, of a levelling sort of topsy-turvy, the lyric anticipates the ensuing dialogue and action.

Yeats provides no description of the principals' costumes either in the stage directions or the play's various drafts. The dialogue strongly suggests that the queen's virginal splendor must be contrasted with the swineherd's half-animal power. That the "foul rags" are not rendered realistically is suggested by the deliberate nonrealism of the dialogue and movement. James Flannery's 1991 Abbey production drew attention to the contrasting appearance of the principals. "While the queen was disturbingly overdressed, buttressed from the world and her own impulses by yards of white cotton, the Swineherd was naked except for a ragged loin cloth. He was made up to appear scratched and torn and bleeding, but not, as Yeats wished, masked. Neither was the queen and, consequently, attention was directed away from the heads of the actors to the muscular, acrobatic movements of the whole body in dance."[22] As Flannery's production demonstrated, masks are not as necessary for the persons in this late play as they were for Bricriu or the Guardian of the Well. What remains essential is the stylization and stillness of the features. This Flannery achieved with mask-like whiteface. As thoroughly steeped as anyone in Yeats's idea of the theater, Flannery in his 1991 production disregarded some of Yeats's stage directions while giving concrete stage life to the images in the play's lyrics. The queen in that production was not discovered "seated and veiled." She was discovered instead high in a niche in the production's surrealistic setting, a wall of skulls. As the combined voices of the attendants sang their final iteration "Crown of gold and dung of swine," she descended by rope to the stage floor. This action anticipated and gave theatrical resonance to the play's final lyric.[23]

> Why must those holy, haughty feet descend
> From emblematic niches, and what hand
> Ran that delicate raddle through their white?
>
> (CPL 396)

This lyric implies that the play's dominant colors must be the white of the queen's "virgin cruelty" and the red of the swineherd's world of dung and sensuality. The stage directions call for the queen's change from white to red after her ritual sacrifice of the swineherd and before she performs to quickening drum taps the dance that, in the penultimate draft, is described as expressing the sexual act.[24] That same draft, a good guide for production, describes her as follows: "Her hands are red. There are red blotches on her. They must not be too realistic—red gloves, red cloths maybe. Some kind of harmony or pattern should suggest blood."[25]

In this draft, one can track the playwright as he seeks the appropriate theatrical resources to express his nonmimetic vision of virgin cruelty and the dung of swine. The severed head with which the queen dances is not described, but, like the heads of Cuchulain's killers in Yeats's final play, this prop should not be realistic. In Flannery's production Sarah-Jane Scaife, as the queen, held "a miniature symbolic severed head in her embrace." In a scarlet dancing-dress, she "lay on the ground and applied its dead lips to her feet, calves, knees, thighs and finally to her groin. She cradled it on her belly, lifted it level to her face and kissed it."[26]

Seated and perfectly still during her opening dialogue, the queen executes precisely chosen movements just before the inner curtain is closed and the offstage execution of the swineherd is carried out:

> I owe my thanks to God that this foul wretch,
> Foul in his rags, his origin, his speech,
> In spite of all his daring, has not dared

5 / THE PLAYWRIGHT AS STAGE MACHINIST

> Ask me to drop my veil. Insulted ears
> Have heard and shuddered, but my face is pure.
> Had it but known the insult of his eyes
> I had torn it with these nails.
>
> (CPL 393)

In her last gesture before the inner curtain is closed, the queen turns toward the swineherd, her back to the audience, and drops her veil. Her pronouncing the death sentence is dramatically fused with the awful daring of a moment's surrender.

In their final exchange, the swineherd and the queen prefigure the nature of the play's subsequent action. The swineherd describes a woman

> That stood all bathed in blood; a drop of blood
> Entered her womb and there begat a child.
> **QUEEN** A severed head; she took it in her hands.
> She stood all bathed in blood. The blood begat.
> O foul, foul, foul!
> **SWINEHERD** She sank in bridal sleep.
> **QUEEN** Her body in that sleep conceived a child.
> Be gone! I shall not see your face again.
>
> (CPL 394)

This play's dramaturgy is such that dialogue invests action with power. Each action is preceded by words whose meaning alters as the subsequent action unfolds. At the same time, the dialogue imparts a new significance to the action that follows it. As the dialogue evolves into dance and lyric, the queen enacts the swineherd's prophecy. She is transformed into a blood-bathed lover who may conceive a blood-begotten child. The second attendant, lending his voice to the swineherd's stylized severed head, laughs and sings. In Worth's production, the audience heard a ventriloquial peal of Dionysiac laughter. The song is a "surrealist nursery rhyme from the depths of the unconscious."[27] It offers a complementary version of murder and transformation. The song's repeated refrain, "A full moon in March" reminds the audience of the season of world-transforming events—of death and transfiguration.

The queen, covered with stylized patterns of red, performs a dance of "frenzied parturition."[28] In a moment of searing irony, her final act with the swineherd's head gives the lie to her final words. A

Full Moon in March exemplifies the fusion of dialogue with movement in Yeats's later plays. The dances are counterpointed by apposite lyric verse, spoken or sung by attendants who at once shadow the principal persons and dilate upon their story. Lyric and movement come together to create complexities of thought and feeling that could be achieved in no other way.

Three of Yeats's five last plays were not performed during his lifetime. *A Full Moon in March*, *The Herne's Egg*, and *The Death of Cuchulain* were so radically inventive in the way they marshaled all the theater's allied arts that they still seem, sixty years after the playwright's death, ahead of their time. Their content was, by some measures, shocking. The eroticism in *A Full Moon in March*,[29] for example, left its 1991 audiences visibly disturbed. It is therefore no surprise that the theater Yeats helped found drew back from these late plays. Unlike Beckett—who in his sixties and seventies became an independent freelance director of his own plays—Yeats always required theatrical collaborators. Because he was unable to gather a group of theater artists to produce these final difficult plays, he bequeathed them to the theater of the future.

The Herne's Egg completed 1937

The Board of the Abbey Theatre rejected *The Herne's Egg* on grounds of obscenity, though one member, in a comic moment consonant with the play's tone, opposed the rejection because the "play was so obscure that no one would know it was obscene." Frank O'Connor recalls that the playwright was "bitterly hurt at the rejection of his beautiful play by a group of non-entities."[30] Seven soldiers violate the priestess of the great Herne god, and the priestess proves that she has not been violated but has, instead, been possessed by her deity. The play moves through shock to apotheosis, as a grotesque gang rape is transmuted into a holy ritual.

The play returns with a vengeance to the brutal farcical mode of *The Green Helmet*. Like Brecht, Hasek, or Heller, writers with whom Yeats is not often compared, the playwright uses farce both to distance his audience from the experience of shocking violence, and to intensify the complex vision of which the violence is a part. "Very personal comedy" (L 524) is a perfect description of *The Herne's Egg*. Full of comic opera soldiers, toy-like props, and a constant threat of grotesque violence, this noisy, brawling play, like the lyric dance plays, evokes a sacred presence and achieves tragic ecstasy.

Attracta is the play's chief agent of the sacred and the ecstatic, and she is introduced amid circumstances that make her appear the comically fanatic follower of a god who might have descended from Cloudcuckooland. The soldiers encounter her with language whose repetitions, at once ludicrous and menacing, anticipate Pinter. Her response, by contrast, is all the more startling in its lyric seriousness.

> **CONGAL**   He and all his principal men
> I and all my principal men
> Take supper at his principal house
> This night in his principal city, Tara;
> And we have set our minds upon
> A certain novelty or relish.
> **MIKE**   Herne's eggs.
> **CONGAL**   This man declares our need. . . .
> **ATTRACTA**   Custom forbids.
> Only the women of these rocks
> Betrothed or married to the Herne,
> The God or ancestor of Hernes,
> Can eat, handle, or look upon those eggs.
>
> (CPL 408)

Attracta's scene effects a transformation through farce to tragic reverie expressed in music, lyric, and dance. The audience hears sounds of this transformation when the tune of the "Great Herne's Feather," first played by the clown Corney, is repeated by a mysterious offstage flute as an otherworldly summons of the god. Attracta's prayer to the Great Herne, one of the play's most memorable lyric passages, establishes her as a figure quite beyond the comprehension of her grotesque interlocutors:

> Strong sinew and soft flesh
> Are foliage round the shaft
> Before the arrowsmith
> Has stripped it, and I pray
> That I, all foliage gone,
> May shoot into my joy.

(CPL 412)

This passage was a favorite of Frank O'Connor's, and he cited it as a far more fitting epitaph for Yeats than the lines that end "Under Ben Bulben."³¹

The scene's astonishing movement away from farce toward tragedy is most evident in Attracta's dance.

> She will move for certain minutes
> As though her god were there
> Thinking how best to move
> A doll upon a wire.
> Then she will move away
> In long leaps as though
> He had remembered his skill.
>
> (CPL 412–13)

The lyric passage directs the dancer to move from grotesque paroxysm to tragic grace. As the god takes possession of his priestess, the mood of the watching girls, who serve as a sort of chorus, changes from unease to awe.

> Those leaps may carry her where
> No woman has gone, . . .
> All I know is that she
> Shall lie there in his bed.
> Nor shall it end until
> She lies there full of his might,
> His thunderbolts in her hand.
>
> (CPL 413)

Attracta's tragic ascent is set amid scenes of farcical stylization. For the first time since *The Countess Cathleen* the playwright abandoned the single setting in favor of a multiscene dramaturgy. During the years that Yeats was at work on this play, Brecht was perfecting a similarly epic structure. This multiscene approach permits, as in Shakespeare, the juxtaposition of disparate tones. Nowhere is the contrast between farce and tragedy more evident than in the first two of the play's six scenes. The opening sequence depicts a stylized, mythically reenacted battle. The contending soldiers move rhythmically, as if in a dance. When swords approach one another, cymbals clash; when swords and shields approach,

5 / THE PLAYWRIGHT AS STAGE MACHINIST

drums boom. The audience is distanced from the violence by these deliberately theatrical sound effects, by the ritual movement, and by the formally stychomythic dialogue.

> **AEDH** Your losses equal mine.
> **CONGAL** They always have and must.
>
> (CPL 406)

The distanced ritual battle partakes of fairy tale, and the "story theater" techniques are reinforced by the nature of the props. The donkey, a symbol of the bestiality that is one of the play's themes, is a life-size child's toy on wheels. The moon of transformation is the "moon of comic tradition" a smiling face.

The brief scene of ritual battle is followed immediately by the scene of Attracta's transmutation. In this scene, the audience is introduced to the toy donkey and to those other bestial symbols, the seven soldiers who will commit the gang rape. One of these proves to be a laconic oracle who parodies both cryptic prophecy and poetic economy. Mike always furnishes the apposite pronouncement while Congal, priest-like or critic-like, offers an interpretive gloss. These devices give Congal and his cohorts a comic air that they will retain through the play's many moods and vicissitudes. The audience remains *verfremdet* estranged from the soldiers' brutal acts by their means of theatrical presentation.

The Brechtian soldiers and the tragic dancer constitute a theatrical apotheosis of the playwright's overarching theme: the battle of the dream with reality. Were Attracta given a more realistic presentation she might be shown, like a Tennessee Williams heroine, to retreat into insanity while the surrounding dogs go on with their doggy life. But this play's unmimetic presentation depicts the dream's complete triumph over reality. Like Cuchulain in Yeats's final play, Attracta makes the truth. There has been no gang rape; instead there has been a divine union with the god. Attracta's utter negation of the soldiers' brute act brings about their devolution and humiliation. The play's subsequent scenes depict Congal's spiritual journey through degradation to a kind of *anagnorisis*. At the last, like Oedipus and Othello, this fallen king is revealed to himself—a revelation that may elicit tragic pity and awe in the audience of this most unusual comedy.

Yeats demonstrates his mastery of the theater and its allied arts as he presents the continuing contrast between the priestess and her tormentors. Attracta stands silent and unmoving as the soldiers' seven ritual blows are struck.

> **MIKE** Seven men.
> (He begins to count, seeming to strike the table with the table-leg, but table and table-leg must not meet. The blow is represented by the sound of the drum.)
> One, two, three, four, five, six, seven men. . . .
> **CONGAL** This man who struck those seven blows
> Means that we seven in the name of the law
> Must handle, penetrate, and possess her.
>
> (CPL 418)

Attracta remains a still and silent image of power that dominates the noisy scene. Her power is augmented by the lyric she sings while the men fling their caps, in order to determine who shall take her first. Her words, punctuated by the thudding caps, make for a startling theatrical sequence:

> When I take a beast
> To my joyful breast
> Though beak and claw I must endure
> Sang the bride of the Herne and the great Herne's bride;
> No lesser life, man bird or beast,
> Can make unblessed what a beast made blessed,
> Can make impure what a beast made pure.
>
> (CPL 419)

Theatrically symmetrical scenes precede and follow the offstage rape. In both scenes, the silent Attracta dominates her noisy, restless antagonists. In both scenes, the priestess lyrically calls upon her god. The scene's devices—the three thunderclaps, the prostrate soldiers, the reluctantly kneeling Congal desperately insisting on the irrelevant fact of rape—figure the king's slow defeat. The final tableau presents the seven violators prostrate at the feet of their victim.

All the battles are choreographed sequences, accompanied by percussion. The creel of precious Herne's eggs is painted on the side of the toy donkey. The bout between the soldiers and the Herne-god's outraged manifestation is mimed. Neither the stones the men throw nor the soaring, wheeling bird are visible to the audience. Amid

5 / THE PLAYWRIGHT AS STAGE MACHINIST

these displays of theatrical pyrotechnics, the real egg that Attracta holds in her hand becomes an anchoring symbol, charged with impenetrable mystery. Thirty-three years before the Abbey Board rejected *The Herne's Egg*, the theater's directors, this time led by Yeats, reluctantly decided not to mount a production of Shaw's *John Bull's Other Island*. One of the characters in this searing exposé of real Irish life longs for a land where the "facts are not brutal and the dreams not unreal." Using the theater's arts, Yeats creates just such a land in this most unShavian comedy.

The brutal effects of battle and rape are lessened by stylization. The weapons, though real, never really clash. No blood, not even stage blood, is shed. The rape is presented in theatrical analogy, first with Mike's pounding table-leg and then with the soldiers' caps hurled at the egg. Yet even these theatrical metaphors are made less brutal by theatrical means. The caps all miss the egg at which they are hurled, and the pounding leg never actually strikes the table. As in all the scenes of violence, the blows are represented by booming drums. Congal and his men are the play's realists, and Yeats takes his revenge on the realists by using theatrical arts to render them less real. At the same time, the egg that becomes Attracta's defining prop retains its reality through all its symbolic avatars. As the surreal action takes its course, reality recedes while the dream acquires reality.

All the theater's tricks are used to substantiate the dream in the play's final scene. Presided over by the unrealistic smiling moon of comic tradition, this is the scene in which the Herne's prophecy that Congal shall meet his death by a fool's hand comes to fruition. Since the realist is entering the world of dream, this scene features a profusion of realistic props: pot, lid, spit, and stones. The stones hurled at the Herne earlier in the play had been mimed, but the stones that are to anchor the spit whose point gives Congal his death wound are real. Even the toy donkey, the play's most spectacularly theatrical prop, acquires a new reality in this scene. Its offstage bray signals Congal's final diminishment.

Katharine Worth, for whom Yeats remains a pathfinder for the modern European theater, brilliantly describes this scene's theatrical virtuosity:

> Two levels of reality there, and now another; the donkey existing in its own right, out there braying its real sound in the 'real' off-stage fields and rocks where a real fate awaits the dead hero. Or may await—but

once we start to speculate on these ideas we are already caught, are investing with the life of our own mind the hard-to-forget world that was created, we know, out of play materials—birds painted on backcloths and life-size toys. . . . The unlikely reality of the donkey in *The Herne's Egg* is the best of signs that Yeats had evolved a theatrical syntax to suit all his needs. . . . for in the theater after all, the dumb wooden donkey is no less real than the off-stage one braying naturalistically; we dissolve one reality into another with the greatest ease, at the touch of a drumbeat, a song, a disconcertingly natural sound.[32]

Central to this scene in which the theater's many modes fuse into a higher reality is the chastened Congal, who now partakes of Attracta's world of dream. In his colloquy with the fool, the king achieves a difficult self-knowledge and an apotheosis that reaches toward tragedy. Like a number of Yeats's heroes, Congal fuses with his opposite. Like many tragic heroes in the Senecan tradition, the king asserts his identity at the last.

> I am King Congal of Conacht and of Tara;
> That wise, victorious, voluble,
> Unlucky, blasphemous,
> Famous, infamous man. . . .
> The great Herne knows that I have won!
>
> (CPL 426)

But in a final moment of theatrical virtuosity, Senecan tragedy is juxtaposed with the hurried and interrupted copulation of French farce. Attracta terrifies Corney with her amorous commands.

> Come lie with me upon the ground.
> Come quickly into my arms—come quickly!
> Come before his body has had time to cool. . . .
> Lie and beget!
>
> (CPL 427)

But Attracta's good intentions are spoiled by the offstage bray. "I thought that I could give a human form / To Congal, but now he must be born a donkey" (CPL 428). For all his Senecan professions, Congal is given another, truer epitaph.

> All that trouble and nothing to show for it;
> Nothing but just another donkey.

5 / THE PLAYWRIGHT AS STAGE MACHINIST   181

(CPL 428)

The Death of Cuchulain completed 1939

Completing the play during his last month, Yeats knew that *The Death of Cuchulain* would not be performed during his lifetime. As with *The Herne's Egg*, he bequeathed to theatrical posterity a blueprint for performance that juggles theatrical modes and radically experiments with ever-shifting relations among dream and reality. Like the other late plays, this play gives theater artists considerable imaginative freedom. Yet the dramatist imposes a Yeatsian discipline on all those who undertake to mount this play, and this seeker after ghosts will haunt any performer, director, or designer who does not heed his guidance.

The first requirement in performance is a "bare stage of any period" (CPL 438). Throughout his playwrighting career, Yeats has been sweeping his stage bare. In the late dance plays, a symbolically painted backcloth provides all the necessary scenery. For this last play, taking place as it does in a sort of dreamscape between life and death, there is not even a suggested background. Objects from the known world would only distract the spectators from the unknown world toward which the action moves. Yeats's last stage is occupied by its people, their words and movements, and the objects they carry with them.

Framed by the antiquated old man and the postmodern street singer, the play is divided into four brief scenes, each dominated by a striking theatrical image. In the first of these, Cuchulain stands on the bare stage between emblems of love and war: Eithne Inguba his mistress and the crow-headed war goddess called the Morigu. The Morigu's appearance is not further described in the stage direction, but a black mask and wings similar in design to those worn by the Guardian of the Well would be effective. Touched by a black wing, the tranced Eithne achieves enlightenment and certainty. For Yeats's old battler, love proves true only when it has been touched by war. Juxtaposing the bright Eithne and the Morigu's raven wing, the playwright uses the theater's real light and shadow to create a living image of this idea.

Cuchulain next encounters Aoife, his ancient enemy and mother to the son he has himself slaughtered. This scene requires an iconic object: the standing stone to which the mortally wounded Cuchulain tries to bind himself. In production, this object can be a large cube like the thrones in *The King of the Great Clock Tower*. In a gesture at once antagonistic and loving, Aoife binds Cuchulain to the stone with her veil, so that he may die upon his feet.

> **AOIFE**   But I am an old woman now, and that
> Your strength may not start up when the time comes,
> I wind my veil about this ancient stone
> And fasten you to it.
> **CUCHULAIN**   But do not spoil your veil.
> Your veils are beautiful, some with threads of gold.
> **AOIFE**   I am too old to care for such things now.
> (She has wound the veil about him.)
>
> (CPL 442)

Aoife's veil wound about the dying hero becomes an emblem for all the amorous and bloody toils, many but not all self-made, in which the old hero has been enmeshed.

The play's central encounter brings Cuchulain face to face with his opposite: the blind man from *On Baile's Strand*. In August, 1938, at his last appearance at the Abbey, the dramatist had been present at a revival of the earlier Cuchulain play, which had shared the bill with the first performance of *Purgatory*. Watching the play with which the Abbey had opened in 1904, Yeats may have been prompted to complete the Cuchulain cycle on which he had been intermittently at work for thirty-five years.[33] In *On Baile's Strand* Cuchulain had described "A brief forgiveness between opposites / That have been hatreds for three times the age / Of this long-stablished ground" (CPL 170). In his last play, Yeats made a theatrical image to figure forth these lines.

Bound to the stone, the mortally wounded hero is immobilized in concentrated stillness. The archetypically antiheroic blind man, groping about Cuchulain's body, feeling for the neck, is shown to be the hero's precise opposite. There can be no starker theatrical contrast than that between the unmoving, upright Cuchulain and the creeping, half-animal, blind man scrabbling about his feet. Yet as is the case with all Yeats's great pairings, these two mutually partake of each other, "live each other's death, die each other's life." When the blind man on a darkened stage, unseen by the audience, slits Cuchulain's throat, the spectators are made to recognize that Cuchulain can have no fitter executioner than his precise antiself.

The queen and the swineherd, Congal and the fool, Cuchulain and the blind man are all variant manifestations of this Yeatsian battle of opposites. In *The Herne's Egg* and in *The Death of Cuchulain,* an unmoving figure is contrasted in his last moments with a chattering, restless antagonist. Ever since he had seen Sarah Bernhardt's Phèdre, Yeats had valued concentrated stillness in the theater. In "The Poet and the Actress" he had adumbrated an effect that his late plays achieve. "We all desire certainty, that is to say that the imagination shall be at rest, no longer troubling about all kinds of things, and no longer bitter; and beauty is the emotion of a soul in the presence of this certainty."[34] Attracta singing to her god as the seven caps fly toward her unviolated Herne's egg and Cuchulain groped by the Blind Man achieve this peculiar Yeatsian beauty in the theater.

But the play does not allow its audience to rest with the certainty that Cuchulain reaches. Emer is introduced in a dance of rage and adoration—adoration of Cuchulain, rage against his killers. Emer interrupts her dance before the stylized, severed heads to listen to the offstage bird notes of Cuchulain's soul taking flight. Then, in a moment of Brechtian shock, the audience is wrenched away from the secret place beyond life and plunged into a contemporary street fair. Cuchulain's effect on twentieth-century Irish turbulence is evoked in the stanzas of the street singer's ballad, the song the harlot sang to the beggar-man:

> What stood in the post-office
> With Pearse and Connoly?
> What comes out of the mountain
> Where men first shed their blood?
> Who thought Cuchulain till it seemed
> He stood where they had stood?
>
> (CPL 446)

In the ballad, the ancient hero fuses with his commemorative statue in the Dublin post office. Ancient and modern music, the soul's flight and the whore's song, dream and reality, all collide in this sequence of total theater.

Yeats most clearly demonstrates his mastery of theatrical resources and theatrical effects in three plays that remained unperformed during his lifetime. The failure of the planned collaboration with Margo Ruddock on *A Full Moon in March* and the Abbey Board's rejection of *The Herne's Egg* may be the last casualties in the dramatist's battle with the elements of drama, with resources of the theater and with theater artists and audiences. His lifetime's war with the theater he both loved and hated burns in every moment of the induction to *The Death of Cuchulain*. But the rage is mitigated and tempered by self-mockery, and even by such implicit, qualified gratitude as is made explicit in "On the Boiler."

> I have aimed at tragic ecstasy, and here and there in my own work and in the work of my friends I have seen it greatly played. What does it matter that it belongs to a dead art and to a time when a man spoke out of an experience and a culture that were not of his time alone, but held his time, as it were, at arm's length, that he might be a spectator of the ages? (EXP 415–16)

The speaker of the induction, who retains some of the playwright's characteristics, pronounces himself as well to be "out of fashion and out of date, like the antiquated romantic stuff the thing is made of." (CPL 438) Yeats knew that his writing for the theater was both ancient as Sophocles and radically innovative. Speaking out of the deepest past, his plays would always belong to the theater of the future. Consequently, his self-mocking surrogate rages against the up-to-date audiences whose imaginations reach neither into the past nor into the future. But the Yeats-like speaker is interrupted, mid-rant, by the offstage piper. "That's from the musicians! I asked them to do that if I was getting excited" (CPL 439). The Yeats of the early Abbey years, who delighted in enemies, would not have mitigated his rage with a puncturing, comic moment; the author of this induction was tempered by a lifetime of conflict with the theater and exultant in his mastery. His ability to laugh while raging suggests that he knew that even this difficult play would find its audience and its time.

Note on Sources

Being blind, I have an unusual relation to books. Of the books I consulted in preparing this study, only Yeats's *Collected Poems and Memoirs* are available in Braille, the former from the Royal National Institute for the Blind, the latter from National Library Service. Yeats's *Collected Plays, Essays and Introductions,* and *Autobiographies* are available on tape from Recording for the Blind and Dyslexic. A few of my secondary sources, Aristotle's *Poetics,* Richard Ellmann's books, and Eric Bentley's important anthology, *The Theory of the Modern Stage,* are also available on tape from RFB and D, an organization that enables thousands of print-handicapped individuals to pursue higher learning. For all the other books and articles referred to in the notes and listed in the bibliography, I used live readers, most of them undergraduates at the University of New Hampshire. In recent years, I have made use of "character recognition" software to transform print documents into machine-readable format.

In the following notes, as well as in the references embedded in the text, I use those sources most readily available to me. For example, while the inkprint pagination for Yeats's *Collected Plays* is available to me, the pagination for the Variorum edition of his plays is not. Whenever I wish to refer to *Variorum Plays,* I must ask a reader to hunt down the page reference—an often time-consuming task. Reader time is infinitely precious to me, and I do not choose to spend more of it than necessary on page hunts. Consequently, whenever I refer to a Yeats play in its final, published version, I use *Collected Plays.* For published variants and notes I use *Variorum Plays.* When I quote from W.S.'s "A Funeral Elegy," I refer to the version posted online to the Shakespeare Electronic Discussion Group, rather than to the version subsequently published.

Several massive new Yeats editions are not yet available to me. The complete text of Allan Wade's selection of letters has been read to me over several years, but I do not yet have access to the multi-volume edition edited by John Kelly and others. I long for the day when publishers will make this collection available on CD-ROM.

Notes

Introduction. *Sightless Insights*

1. James Flannery, "W. B. Yeats, Gordon Craig, and the Visual Arts of the Theatre" in Robert O'Driscoll and Lorna Reynolds, eds. *Yeats and the Theatre* (Niagara Falls, NY: Maclean, 1976), 82.
2. Anthony Roche, "Lady Gregory: Whose Drama Is It Anyway?" Lecture delivered at the Yeats International Summer School, Sligo, 8 August 1997.
3. James Pethica, "'Our Kathleen': Yeats's Collaboration with Lady Gregory in the Writing of *Cathleen ni Houlihan*" in Deirdre Toomey, ed. *Yeats and Women* (New York: St. Martin's Press, 1997), 205–22; see especially 216–17.
4. T. S. Eliot, "Yeats" in John Unterecker, ed. *Yeats: A Collection of Critical Essays* (Englewood Cliffs, NJ: Prentice-Hall, 1963), 62.
5. W[illiam] S[hakespeare], "A Funeral Elegy for Master William Peter" (London: G. Eld for T. Horpe, 1612). Normalized text, ed. D. Foster, ll. 257–64.
6. Katharine Worth, *The Irish Drama of Europe from Yeats to Beckett* (Atlantic Highlands, NJ: Humanities Press, 1978), 158.
7. Ben Jonson, *The Staple of News* in *The Complete Plays of Ben Jonson* II (London: J. M. Dent, 1970), 349.
8. E. Gordon Craig, "The Art of the Theatre" in Eric Bentley, ed. *The Theory of the Modern Stage* (Harmonsworth: Penguin, 1968), 115.
9. Sylvia C. Ellis, *The Plays of W. B. Yeats: Yeats and the Dancer* (New York: St. Martin's Press, 1995), 340.
10. R. F. Foster, *W. B. Yeats: A Life*, vol. 1, *The Apprentice Mage* (New York: Oxford University Press, 1997), 340.

Chapter 1: *The Problem of Personality*

1. W. B. Yeats, "Three Lectures on Personality" in Robert O'Driscoll and Lorna Reynolds, eds. *Yeats and the Theatre* (Niagara Falls, NY: Maclean, 1976), 21–22.
2. Anna Macbride White and A. Norman Jeffares, eds. *The Gonne-Yeats Letters 1893–1938* (New York: Norton, 1992), 151.

3. Georg Lukacs, "The Sociology of Modern Drama" in Eric Bentley, ed. *The Theory of the Modern Stage* (Harmonsworth: Penguin, 1968), 426.

4. White and Jeffares, 151.

5. Bernard Shaw, "The Problem Play: A Symposium" in E. J. West, ed. *Shaw on Theatre* (New York: Hill and Wang, 1958), 54.

6. Una Ellis-Fermor, *The Irish Dramatic Movement* (London: Methuen, 1939), ix–x.

7. Pethica in Toomey, 205–22.

8. Lukacs in Bentley, 426.

9. Ibid., 431; 434–35.

10. O'Driscoll & Reynolds, 19.

11. Ibid., 18.

12. L. A. G. Strong, "William Butler Yeats" in Stephen Gwynn, ed. *William Butler Yeats: Essays in Tribute* (Port Washington, NY: Kennikat Press, 1965), 221–22; first published 1940 as *Scattering Branches*.

13. Richard Ellmann: *Yeats: The Man and the Masks* (New York: Dutton, 1948), 182.

14. Aristotle, *Poetics*, Trans. S. H. Butcher, (New York: Hill and Wang, 1961), 63.

15. O'Driscoll and Reynolds, 17–18.

16. E. M. Pinciss, "A Dancer for Mr. Yeats" in *Educational Theatre Journal*, Fall, 1969, 387–88; and Sylvia C. Ellis, *The Plays of W. B. Yeats: Yeats and the Dancer* (New York: St. Martin's Press, 1995), 226–27.

17. David Magarshack, "Stanislavsky" in Eric Bentley, ed. *The Theory of the Modern Stage* (Harmonsworth: Penguin, 1968), 220–21; 238–39.

18. Adrian Frazier, *Behind the Scenes: Yeats, Horniman, and the Struggle for the Abbey Theatre* (Berkeley: University of California Press, 1990), 16.

19. Aristotle, 64.

20. Frazier, 16.

21. O'Driscoll and Reynolds, 24.

22. Padriac Colum, "Preface" in Maire nic Shiublaigh, *The Splendid Years* (Dublin: James Duffy, 1955), vii–viii.

23. Quoted in Augusta Gregory, *Our Irish Theatre* (n.p., 1914; reprint, New York: Capricorn, 1965), 106.

24. Lukacs in Bentley, 429.

25. Ann Saddlemyer, ed. *Theatre Business: The Correspondence of the First Abbey Directors: William Butler Yeats, Lady Gregory and J. M. Synge* (University Park, PA: The Pennsylvania State University Press, 1982), 179.

26. Ibid., *Theatre Business* 206.

27. Ibid., 174.

28. S. B. Bushrui, *Yeats's Verse Plays: The Revisions 1900–1910* (New York: Clarendon Press, 1965), 154.

29. Ellis-Fermor, 113.

30. Ibid., 115.

31. Bushrui, 154.

32. Lennox Robinson, "The Man and the Dramatist" in Gwynn, 90.

33. O'Driscoll and Reynolds, 54.

34. Ibid., see especially 53–55.

35. Ibid., 80.
36. Curtis Baker Bradford, *Yeats At Work* (Carbondale: Southern Illinois University Press, 1965), 185.
37. Sean O'Casey, *Autobiographies* II, (London: Macmillan, 1963), 233.

Chapter 2. *Writing for the Ear*

1. Edmund Wilson, *Axel's Castle: A Study in the Imaginative Literature of 1870–1930* (New York: Charles Scribner's Sons, 1953, first published 1931), 36.
2. White and Jeffares, 283.
3. Aristotle, 63.
4. David R. Clark and James D. McGuire, eds. *W. B. Yeats, The Writing of "Sophocles' King Oedipus": Manuscripts of W. B. Yeats* (Philadelphia: American Philosophical Society, 1989), 46–47.
5. Clark and McGuire, 189–90.
6. Ibid., 74–75.
7. Richard Taylor, "Metrical Variation in Yeats's Verse" in Warwick Gould, ed. *Yeats Annual* 8 (London: Macmillan, 1991), 21–22; 29–30; and Derek Attridge, *The Rhythms of English Poetry* (London: Longman, 1982), 70–74. Unfortunately for me, the system of notation used herein does not lend itself to the blind; thus, while I recognize its usefulness, I cannot make good use of it. In describing the metric qualities of the songs in the dance plays, I will need to refer to sound and the ear rather than to a more precise graphical notation that attempts to describe what the ear hears in terms of what the eye sees.
8. Bradford, 181.
9. Ibid., 184.
10. Ibid., 191. See also James Longenbach, *Stone Cottage: Pound, Yeats, and Modernism* (New York: Oxford University Press, 1988), 214 and Taylor in *Yeats Annual* 8, 30.
11. Bradford, 177.
12. Ibid., 177.
13. Ibid., 177.
14. Aristotle, 87.
15. Bradford, 297.
16. Ibid., 298–99.
17. Ibid., 300.

Chapter 3. *Reshaping the Plot*

1. Gregory, *Our Irish Theatre* 101–2.
2. Aristotle, 63.
3. White and Jeffares, 175.
4. Lukacs, in Bentley, 436.
5. David R. Clark, *W. B. Yeats and the Theatre of Desolate Reality* Rev. ed. (Washington, D.C.: Catholic University of America Press, 1993), 117.

6. Ellmann, 182.
7. O'Driscoll and Reynolds, 53–55.
8. Karen Dorn, *Players and Painted Stage; The Theatre of W. B. Yeats* (Totowa, NJ: Barnes and Noble, 1984), 10–11.
9. Bradford, 169.
10. Aristotle, 69.
11. Longenbach, 202.
12. Ibid., 197–98.
13. Taylor in O'Driscoll and Reynolds, 137–40.
14. Helen Vendler, *Yeats's Vision and the Later Plays* (Cambridge: Harvard University Press, 1963), 221.
15. W. B. Yeats, "The Poet and the Actress" in Clark, 175.
16. Vendler, 230.
17. Ibid., 231.
18. Clark, 213–14; and Bradford, 236.
19. Robinson in Gwynn, ed., 112.
20. Bradford, 220, 234.
21. Ibid., 219–22.
22. Eliot in Unterecker, 61.
23. Sandra F. Siegel, ed. *Purgatory: Manuscript Materials Including the Author's Final Text* (Ithaca: Cornell University Press, 1986), 47–48.
24. Ibid., 53.
25. Ibid., 24–25.
26. Ibid., 58–59.
27. Eliot, "Yeats" in Unterecker, 59.
28. Peter Ure, *Yeats the Playwright* (Totowa, NJ: Barnes and Noble, 1963), 109–10.
29. Arthur Symons, *The Symbolist Movement in Literature* (New York: E. P. Dutton, 1919, first published 1898), xix.
30. Eric Bentley, *The Playwright as Thinker* (New York: Harcourt Brace and World, 1967, first published 1947), 127.

Chapter 4. *Opinions and Ideas*

1. Richard Ellmann, *The Identity of Yeats* (New York: Oxford University Press, 1964), 295–96.
2. Aristotle, 62.
3. Ellmann, *The Identity of Yeats*, 88.
4. Foster, 295.
5. Henri Bergson, "Laughter" in Wylie Sypher, ed. *Comedy* (Garden City, NY: Doubleday, 1956), 66–67.
6. Bushrui, 111–112.
7. Ure, 35.
8. Heinz Kosok, "Ireland's Silvery Shadow: Sean O'Casey's Critical Debate with W. B. Yeats," Lecture delivered at Yeats International Summer School, Sligo, 7 August 1997.

9. Curtis Baker Bradford, *Yeats At Work,* 234.
10. Curtis Baker Bradford, *The Writing of "The Player Queen" Manuscripts of W. B. Yeats* (Dekalb, IL: Northern Illinois University Press, 1977), 45.
11. Ibid., 123–24.
12. Ibid., 43.
13. Ibid., 127.
14. Ibid., 160.
15. Ibid., 114–15.
16. Ibid., 375.
17. Liam Miller, *The Noble Drama of W. B. Yeats* (Dublin: Dolmen Press, 1977), 291.
18. Ibid., 291.
19. Bradford, *Yeats At Work,* 262.
20. Phillip L. Marcus, ed. *The Death of Cuchulain, Manuscript Materials Including the Author's Final Text* (Ithaca: Cornell University Press, 1982), 11.

Chapter 5. *The Playwright as Stage Machinist*

1. Foster, 295.
2. Ibid., 289.
3. Ibid., 364–65.
4. Saddlemyer, *Theatre Business,* 139.
5. Ibid., 205.
6. Ibid., 139.
7. Ursula Bridge, ed. *W. B. Yeats and T. Sturge Moore: Their Correspondence 1901–1937* (New York: Oxford University Press, 1953), 5–7.
8. William M. Murphy, *Family Secrets: William Butler Yeats and his Relatives* (Syracuse: Syracuse University Press, 1995), 175.
9. James Knowlson, *Damned to Fame: The Life of Samuel Beckett* (New York: Simon and Schuster, 1996), 447.
10. James Flannery, "W. B. Yeats, Gordon Craig, and the Visual Arts of the Theatre" in Robert O'Driscoll and Lorna Reynolds, eds. *Yeats and the Theatre* (Niagara Falls, N.Y.: Maclean, 1976), 84; my italics.
11. E. Gordon Craig, "The Art of the Theatre" in Eric Bentley, ed. *The Theory of the Modern Stage* (Harmonsworth: Penguin, 1968), 115.
12. Ann Saddlemyer, "The Heroic Discipline of the Looking-Glass" in Robin Skelton and Ann Saddlemyer, eds. *The World of W. B. Yeats* (Seattle: University of Washington Press, 1965), 69.
13. Ibid., 69.
14. Longenbach, 218.
15. Worth, 153.
16. Frazier, 16.
17. Clark, *W. B. Yeats and the Theatre of Desolate Reality,* 139–40.
18. W. B. Yeats, "The Poet and the Actress" in Clark, 175.
19. Ibid., 171–72.

20. Pinciss, 389.
21. Ibid., 389–91.
22. Ellis, 339.
23. Ibid., 338–39.
24. Curtis Baker Bradford, *Yeats At Work,* 288.
25. Ibid., 287.
26. Ellis, 339.
27. Worth, 117–18.
28. W. B. Yeats, "The Poet and the Actress" in Clark, 171.
29. Ellis, 340.
30. Frank O'Connor, *My Father's Son* (New York: Knopf, 1969), 224–25.
31. O'Connor, 227–28.
32. Worth, 70.
33. Liam Miller, *The Noble Drama of W. B. Yeats* (Dublin: Dolmen Press, 1977), 305.
34. W. B. Yeats, "The Poet and the Actress" in Clark, 180.

Bibliography

Alspach, Russell K. ed. *The Variorum Edition of the Plays of W. B. Yeats.* New York: Macmillan, 1966.

Aristotle. *Poetics.* Translated by S. H. Butcher. New York: Hill and Wang, 1961.

Attridge, Derek. *The Rhythms of English Poetry.* London: Longman, 1982.

Bentley, Eric. *The Playwright as Thinker.* New York: Harcourt Brace and World, 1967.

Bentley, Eric, ed. *The Theory of the Modern Stage.* Harmonsworth: Penguin, 1968.

Bergson, Henri. "Laughter." in *Comedy.* Edited by Wylie Sypher, 61–192. Garden City, NY: Doubleday, 1956.

Bradford, Curtis Baker. *The Writing of "The Player Queen" Manuscripts of W. B. Yeats.* Dekalb, IL: Northern Illinois University Press, 1977.

Bradford, Curtis Baker. *Yeats At Work.* Carbondale: Southern Illinois University Press, 1965.

Bridge, Ursula, ed. *W. B. Yeats and T. Sturge Moore: Their Correspondence 1901–1937.* New York: Oxford University Press, 1953.

Bushrui, S. B. *Yeats's Verse Plays: The Revisions 1900–1910.* New York: Clarendon Press, 1965.

Clark, David R. *W. B. Yeats and the Theatre of Desolate Reality* Rev. ed. Washington, DC: Catholic University of America Press, 1993.

Clark, David R. and James D. McGuire, eds. *W. B. Yeats, The Writing of Sophocles' "King Oedipus": Manuscripts of W. B. Yeats.* Philadelphia: American Philosophical Society, 1989.

Craig, E. Gordon. *On the Art of the Theatre.* New York: Theatre Arts Books, 1960.

Dorn, Karen. *Players and Painted Stage; The Theatre of W. B. Yeats.* Totowa, NJ: Barnes and Noble, 1984.

Ellis, Sylvia C. *The Plays of W. B. Yeats: Yeats and the Dancer.* New York: St. Martin's Press, 1995.

Ellis-Fermor, Una. *The Irish Dramatic Movement.* London: Methuen, 1939.

Ellmann, Richard. *The Identity of Yeats.* New York: Oxford University Press, 1964.

———. *Yeats: The Man and the Masks.* New York: Dutton, 1948.

Flannery, James W. *W. B. Yeats and the Idea of a Theater: The Early Abbey Theatre in Theory and Practice.* New Haven: Yale University Press, 1976.

Foster, Donald, ed. "A Funeral Elegy for Master William Peter by W[illiam] S[hakespeare]." In SHAKSPER file server. Available from Listserv@WS.Bowie.State.edu; INTERNET.

Foster, R. F. *W. B. Yeats: A Life:* Vol. 1, *The Apprentice Mage.* New York: Oxford University Press, 1997.

Frazier, Adrian. *Behind the Scenes: Yeats, Horniman, and the Struggle for the Abbey Theatre.* Berkeley: University of California Press, 1990.

Friedman, Barton R. *Adventures in the Deeps of the Mind: The Cuchulain Cycle of W. B. Yeats.* Princeton: Princeton University Press, 1977.

Gould, Warwick, ed. *Yeats Annual* 8. London: Macmillan, 1991.

Gregory, Augusta. *Cuchulain of Muirthemne.* New York: Oxford University Press, 1970.

———. *Our Irish Theatre.* New York: Capricorn, 1965.

Gwynn, Stephen, ed. *William Butler Yeats: Essays in Tribute.* Port Washington, NY: Kennikat Press, 1965.

Jonson, Ben. *The Complete Plays.* London: J. M. Dent, 1970.

Knowlson, James. *Damned to Fame: The Life of Samuel Beckett.* New York: Simon and Schuster, 1996.

Kosok, Heinz. "Ireland's Silvery Shadow: Sean O'Casey's Critical Debate with W. B. Yeats." Lecture delivered at Yeats International Summer School, Sligo, 7 August 1997.

Longenbach, James. *Stone Cottage: Pound, Yeats, and Modernism.* New York: Oxford University Press, 1988.

Lukacs, Georg. "The Sociology of Modern Drama." In *The Theory of the Modern Stage,* edited by Eric Bentley, 425–55. Harmonsworth: Penguin, 1968.

Marcus, Phillip L. ed. *The Death of Cuchulain: Manuscript Materials Including the Author's Final Text.* Ithaca and London: Cornell University Press, 1982.

Miller, Liam. *The Noble Drama of W. B. Yeats.* Dublin: Dolmen Press, 1977.

Murphy, William M. *Family Secrets: William Butler Yeats and his Relatives.* Syracuse: Syracuse University Press, 1995.

nic Shiublaigh, Maire. *The Splendid Years.* Dublin: James Duffy, 1955.

O'Casey, Sean. *Autobiographies* II. London: Macmillan, 1963.

O'Connor, Frank. *My Father's Son.* New York: Knopf, 1969.

O'Driscoll, Robert, and Lorna Reynolds, eds. *Yeats and the Theatre.* Niagara Falls, NY: Maclean, 1976.

Oppel, Frances Nesbitt. *Mask and Tragedy: Yeats and Nietzsche, 1902–10.* Charlottesville: University Press of Virginia, 1987.

Pinciss, E. M. "A Dancer for Mr. Yeats." in *Educational Theatre Journal,* Vol. 20, Fall, 1969, (Washington, DC: American Theatre Association), 386–93.

Roche, Anthony. "Lady Gregory: Whose Drama Is It Anyway?" Lecture delivered at the Yeats International Summer School, Sligo, 8 August 1997.

Saddlemyer, Ann, ed. *Theatre Business; The Correspondence of the First Abbey Directors: William Butler Yeats, Lady Gregory and J. M. Synge.* University Park: The Pennsylvania State University Press, 1982.

Shaw, Bernard. "The Problem Play: A Symposium." in *Shaw on Theatre*. Edited by E. J. West, 53–61. New York: Hill and Wang, 1958.

Siegel, Sandra F. ed. *Purgatory: Manuscript Materials Including the Author's Final Text*. Ithaca: Cornell University Press, 1986.

Skelton, Robin, and Ann Saddlemyer, eds. *The World of W. B. Yeats*. Seattle: University of Washington Press, 1965.

Skene, Reg. *The Cuchulain Plays of W. B. Yeats: A Study*. New York: Columbia University Press, 1974.

Steinman, Michael. *Yeats's Heroic Figures: Wilde, Parnell, Swift, Casement*. Albany: State University of New York Press, 1983.

Symons, Arthur. *The Symbolist Movement in Literature*. New York: E. P. Dutton, 1919.

Taylor, Richard. *The Drama of W. B. Yeats: Irish Myth and the Japanese Noh*. New Haven: Yale University Press, 1976.

———. "Metrical Variation in Yeats's Verse." in *Yeats Annual* 8. Edited by Warwick Gould, 20–38. London: Macmillan, 1991.

Toomey, Deirdre, ed. *Yeats and Women*. New York: St. Martin's Press, 1997.

Unterecker, John, ed. *Yeats: A Collection of Critical Essays*. Englewood Cliffs, NJ: Prentice-Hall, 1963.

Ure, Peter. *Yeats the Playwright*. Totowa, N.J.: Barnes and Noble, 1963.

Vendler, Helen. *Yeats's Vision and the Later Plays*. Cambridge: Harvard University Press, 1963.

Wade, Allan, ed. *The Letters of W. B. Yeats*. London: Hart-Davis, 1954.

White, Anna Macbride, and A. Norman Jeffares, eds. *The Gonne-Yeats Letters 1893–1938*. New York: Norton, 1992.

Wilde, Oscar. *The Artist as Critic: Critical Writings of Oscar Wilde*. Edited by Richard Ellmann. New York: Random House, 1969.

Wilson, Edmund. *Axel's Castle: A Study in the Imaginative Literature of 1870–1930*. New York: Charles Scribner's Sons, 1953.

Worth, Katharine. *The Irish Drama of Europe from Yeats to Beckett*. Atlantic Highlands, NJ: Humanities Press, 1978.

Yeats, W. B. *Autobiographies*. London: Macmillan, 1955.

———. *Collected Plays*. London: Macmillan, 1962.

———. *Collected Poems*. London: Macmillan, 1961.

———. *Essays and Introductions*. London: Macmillan, 1961.

———. *Explorations*. London: Macmillan, 1962.

———. *Memoirs*, edited by Denis Donoghue. New York: Macmillan, 1972.

———. *Mythologies*. London: Macmillan, 1959.

———. *A Vision Reissue with the Author's Final Revisions*. New York: Macmillan, 1965.

Index

Abbey Theatre, 19, 37, 64, 65, 66, 86, 87, 88, 91, 92, 110, 122, 125, 145, 147, 152, 153, 158, 163, 165–68, 170, 171, 174, 179, 182, 184
Adelphi, 145
"Advice to Playwrights," 86
Ainlee, Henry, 157
"All Souls' Night," 121
Allgood, Sarah, 32
Antony and Cleopatra, 52, 53, 116
Aristotle, 22–23, 24, 36, 40–41, 60, 84, 86–87, 93, 94, 123
Artaud, Antonin, 20, 22
At the Hawk's Well, 20, 38, 48, 49, 55–57, 65, 66, 68–74, 82, 102–4, 109, 157
Attridge, Derek, 69
"Autobiography, First Draft," 40
Avenue Theatre, 115

Beaumont, Francis, 33
Beckett, Samuel, 101, 109, 152, 155, 168, 169, 174
Beerbohm, Max, 128
Bentley, Eric, 120
Bergson, Henri, 131
Bernhardt, Sarah, 20, 183
Bradford, Curtis Baker, 73, 84, 101, 108, 110, 112, 125, 135, 147
Brand, 119
Brecht, Bertolt, 158, 174, 176, 177, 183
Browning, Robert, 102
Bruce, Brenda, 155
"Byzantium," 38, 103

Campbell, Mrs. Patrick: and *Deirdre*, 18, 50, 99, 101; and *The Player Queen*, 136
Cat and the Moon, The, 164
Cathleen ni Houlihan, 19, 28–35, 37, 40, 122, 153
"Certain Noble Plays of Japan," 38
Chapman, Derek, 167
"Circus Animals' Desertion, The," 38
Clark, David R., 65, 108, 166, 167
Colum, Padraic, 44, 51, 52
Comedia del Arte, 36–37
Countess Cathleen, The, 39–41, 43, 135, 151, 160–68
Craig, E. Gordon: and *The Countess Cathleen*, 160; and dance plays, 156; and disagreements with Yeats, 22, 155–56; and distrust of words, 20, 22, 155–56; and *The Hourglass*, 155, 156; and masks, 156–57; and *On Baile's Strand*, 156; and *The Player Queen*, 138, 155; and *Vikings of Helgaland*, 156
Cuchulain of Muirthemne, 47, 87–88, 94–95, 96–97
"Cuchulain's Fight with the Sea," 47–48, 91

Darragh, Florence, 49–50, 154
Death of Cuchulain, The, 17, 116, 123, 149–51, 164, 174, 181–84
"Dialogue of Self and Soul, A," 17, 38
Deirdre, 18, 36, 43, 49–55, 86, 94–101, 102, 103, 104, 110, 116

Deirdre of the Sorrows, 38, 52–53, 160
Doll's House, A, 31
"Dramatis Personae," 162–63
Dreaming of the Bones, The, 66, 74–83, 104, 109, 115, 167
Dulac, Edmund, 38, 157

"Easter, 1916," 66, 69, 80, 131
Eliot, T. S., 20, 69, 115, 118, 157
Ellis, Sylvia, 22
Ellis-Fermor, Una, 32, 51, 52
Ellmann, Richard, 36, 48
Emperor and Galilean, 119

Farr, Florence, 162–63
Father, The, 113
Faust, 64
Fay, Frank: and Abbey Theatre, 50, 155; and *On Baile's Strand*, 44–45, 89
Fay, William, 18, 90
Fenollosa, Ernest, 38, 156
Fighting the Waves, 18, 20, 169
Flannery, James, 18, 22, 169, 171–72
Fletcher, John, 33
Fo, Dario, 158
Foster, R. F., 22
Four Plays for Dancers, 58, 69
Frazier, Adrian, 40, 41, 161
Full Moon in March, A, 22, 23–24, 58, 170–74, 183, 184
"Funeral Elegy, A," 21

Galsworthy, John, 34, 36, 112
Ghost Sonata, 166
Ghosts, 115, 119
Goethe, Johann Wolfgang von, 149
Golden Bough, The, 147
Gonne, Maud: and *Cathleen ni Houlihan*, 28, 29–30, 31–32; and *The Countess Cathleen*, 40; and Jubilee riots, 31; and *On Baile's Strand*, 90; and opinion, 121–22; and poems, 59
Green Helmet, The, 103, 141, 158–60, 174
Gregory, Augusta: and Abbey Theatre, 152, 153–54; and *Cathleen ni Houlihan*, 19, 33, 35; and Chicago Little Theatre, 152; and *Cuchulain of Muirthemne*, 47, 87–88, 89, 90, 91, 93, 94–95, 96–97, 98, 99–100, 102, 114; and *Deirdre*, 49–50; and folklore, 18; and Nobel Address, 19; and *On Baile's Strand*, 47, 90, 93; and *The Only Jealousy of Emer*, 104–5, 106; and theatrical correspondence, 37, 154, 156; and *Where There is Nothing*, 123
Grotowski, Jerzy, 20

Hamlet, 45, 49, 116, 134
Happy Days, 152, 155, 168, 169
Hasek, Jaroslav, 174
Hedda Gabler, 120
Heller, Joseph, 174
Herne's Egg, The, 164, 174–80, 183, 184
Hollinshed, Raphael, 87
Holloway, Joseph, 146, 154–55, 170
Hourglass, The, 123–28, 155, 156, 168
Hyde, Douglas, 123

Ibsen, Henrik, 43, 58, 108, 119–20, 156, 164–65
Irish National Theatre, 86, 125
"Introduction to my Plays, An," 59
Itow, Michio, 20, 38

John Bull's Other Island, 179
Johnson, Samuel, 109
Jonson, Ben, 21
Joyce, James, 128, 153
Jubilee riots, 31
Justice, 34–35, 36, 112

King Lear, 134, 168
King of the Great Clock Tower, The, 23–24, 168–70, 181
King's Threshold, The, 36, 43, 123, 128–33, 137
Knowlson, James, 155

Land of Heart's Desire, The, 115, 155
Lectures on Personality, 39, 53
London Zoo, 38, 55
Longenbach, James, 73
Lukács, Georg, 29, 33–34, 35, 47, 93

Macbeth, 45, 46
MacCormack, F. J., 170
Maeterlinck, Maurice, 169
Mann, Thomas, 29
Marcus, Phillip, 151
Marlowe, Christopher, 62, 78
Marx Brothers, 159
Mask, The, 157
McGuire, James, 65
McNamara, Brinsley, 140
"Meditations in Time of Civil War," 133
"Meru," 124
Middleton, Thomas, 51
Midsummer Night's Dream, A, 31
Miller, Liam, 146
Monck, Nugent, 125, 155, 160, 165
Moore, George, 28, 29
"Mother of God, The," 21

Nazis, 118–19
Nietzsche, Friedrich, 129, 130, 133
"Nineteen Hundred and Nineteen," 133
"No Second Troy," 82
Nobel Prize for Literature, 18–19
Noh Drama, 38, 44, 48, 55, 102, 156
North, Sir Thomas, 87

O'Casey, Sean, 57, 133–35, 137
O'Connor, Frank, 174, 176
O'Neill, Maire, 38
"Old Stone Cross, The," 27
On Baile's Strand, 17, 36, 43, 44–49, 86, 87–94, 156, 182
"On the Boiler," 51, 117, 144–45, 184
Only Jealousy of Emer, The, 23, 57–58, 61–64, 104–8, 167
Othello, 177

"Per Amica Silentia Lunae," 136, 151
Pethica, James, 33
Phédre, 183
Pinter, Harold, 175
Playboy of the Western World, The, 153
Player Queen, The, 123, 136–44, 145, 150, 155
Plough and the Stars, The, 133

Plunkett, Horace, 122
"Poet and the Actress, The," 183
Poetics, 22–23, 152
Pound, Ezra, 18, 38, 101–2, 156
Purgatory, 58, 65, 83–85, 114–20, 167

Racine, Jean, 22, 48, 87
Red Branch Cycle, 87, 102, 114
Resurrection, The, 123, 145–49
"Reveries Over Childhood and Youth," 121
Richard II, 168
Riders to the Sea, 152
Robinson, Lennox, 52–53
Romeo and Juliet, 27, 53
Rosmersholm, 115, 119
Ruddock, Margo, 184
Russell, George, (A. E.) 22, 119

Salome, 154
Scaife, Sarah-Jane, 172
Second Mrs. Tanqueray, The, 50
Seneca, 180
Shadowy Waters, The, 35, 41–43, 48, 49, 57, 86
Shakespeare, Olivia, 134
Shakespeare, William, 20, 21, 35, 48, 61, 62, 87, 108–9, 134, 176
Shaw, George Bernard, 31, 58, 123, 179
Sidhe, 56, 57
Siegel, Sandra, 117
Silver Tassie, The, 133–35
"Sociology of Modern Drama, The," 29
Sophocles, 22, 48, 87, 94, 105, 117, 119, 184
Sophocles' *King Oedipus*, 64–68, 72, 116, 117, 177
Spenser, Edmund, 39
Spreading the News, 87
Stanislavsky, Konstantin, 39, 44
Strindberg, August, 113, 166, 169
Strong, L. A. G., 35, 48
Swift, Jonathan, 108, 109, 135
Symons, Arthur, 41–42, 86, 119, 120

Synge, John Millington: and Abbey Theatre, 153–54; and art as collaboration, 18; and *Deirdre*, 49–50; and *Deirdre of the Sorrows*, 52–53, 96; and Nobel Address, 18–19; and *The Playboy of the Western World*, 153; and prose dialogue, 74, 75; and *Riders to the Sea*, 152

Taylor, Richard, 69, 73, 102
Tempest, The, 109
Tiresias, 17
Tower, The, 58
"Tragic Theatre, The," 55
"Trembling of the Veil, The," 31
Trinity Repertory, 94

"Under Ben Bulben," 176
United Irishman, 131
Ure, Peter, 119

Valois, Ninette de: and *Fighting the Waves*, 18, 20, 169; and *King of the Great Clock Tower, The*, 20, 169, 170

Vendler, Helen, 107
Vikings of Helgaland, 156
Vision, A, 141–42, 145

Waiting for Godot, 152, 159
"Wanderings of Oisin, The," 87
Waters of Immortality, The, 102
When We Dead Awaken, 119, 164–65
Where There is Nothing, 123, 124, 137
Wilde, Oscar, 52
Williams, Tennessee, 177
Wilson, Edmund, 59
Wind Among the Reeds, The, 164
Winding Stair, The, 58
Words Upon the Window Pane, The, 58, 108–14, 115, 120
Worth, Katharine, 21, 169, 173

Yeats, George, 18, 141
Yeats International Summer School, 167
Yeats, J. B., 23, 27, 28, 50, 93, 121, 153

OHIO UNIVERSITY LIBRARY
Please return this book as soon as you have finished with it. In order to avoid a fine it must be returned by the latest date stamped below. All books are subject to recall after two weeks or immediately if needed for reserve.

CF